the driving people

Electric Cars
– The Future is Now!

Your guide to the cars you can buy now
and what the future holds

Also from Veloce Publishing –

The Efficient Driver's Handbook – Your guide to fuel efficient driving techniques and car choice (Moss)
Roads with a View – England's greatest views and how to find them by road (Corfield)

www.rac.co.uk
www.veloce.co.uk

This publication has been produced on behalf of RAC by Veloce Publishing Ltd. The views and the opinions expressed by the author are entirely his own, and do not necessarily reflect those of RAC. New automotive technology is constantly emerging; the information in this book reflects the status quo at the date of publication.

First published in August 2010 by Veloce Publishing Limited, Veloce House, Parkway Farm Business Park, Middle Farm Way, Poundbury, Dorchester, Dorset, DT1 3AR, England.
Fax 01305 250479/e-mail info@veloce.co.uk/web www.veloce.co.uk or www.velocebooks.com.

Front cover picture: Mega City 'refuelling' courtesy Nice Car Company.

ISBN: 978-1-845843-10-6 UPC: 6-36847-04310-0

the driving people

Electric Cars
– The Future is Now!

Your guide to the cars you can buy now and what the future holds

Arvid Linde

Contents

Foreword & Introduction

Foreword

Environmentalists, politicians and car manufacturers all agree on one thing - electric cars are coming. Opinions on time scales, benefits, infrastructure and the technology under the bonnet may differ, but they do agree that they are a key part of motoring's future.

We at RAC are committed to helping motorists understand and make the most of new fuels and technologies to improve their driving experience. This book will hopefully educate a wider audience about the potential of these new vehicles.

For more information about the RAC's views on alternative fuel sources, please read our latest report on motoring at www.rac.co.uk

RAC

Introduction

Hello, there. Let me introduce myself. I'm an electric car and I'll be a part of your lives very soon. I was king of the road in the early 20th century in the USA, before being knocked off my pedestal by Henry Ford's mass motoring campaign. I'm back, though, after more than 80 years, stronger than ever.

The internal combustion engine of my fiercest competitor has around 100 moving parts (in some cases more) while I've got ... well ... one – a rotor that rotates inside a stator. Imagine all the friction, rattle and energy loss that 100 parts create, rotating or reciprocating simultaneously. I've got none of that, and, due to the specifics of electric motors, I produce almost constant power and torque regardless of revs. That brings us to another interesting matter: I can do without a sophisticated gearbox. Just a simple single-speed reduction gear is enough to keep me from going too fast. And I like going fast – after all, the first car to break the coveted 100kmh (62mph) speed barrier in 1899 was an electric car driven by Belgian speed-fanatic Camille Jenatzy.

I'm run on pure electricity that is stored in battery packs under my floor. My younger cousin, the hybrid car, has both an electric motor and a petrol/gasoline engine on-board. This lets him cover longer distances, but also makes him less efficient.

Because electricity is much cheaper than petrol, and because I'm more efficient than a gas-guzzler, I can save you up to 85 per cent on your travel bill. Besides, as the government thinks I'm a zero-emissions vehicle (don't tell them I'm not, please) they will waive the road tax, and even pay you money (in tax incentives) to drive me.

I'm nothing like my granny the milk float, bless her soul. She's still the heart of the community in some places, and we can all forgive her being a wee bit slow. I'm fun to drive, quick to accelerate, and responsive to commands. If you keep your foot on the throttle, I'll run out of 'juice' pretty soon, though, and you'll have to push me back home or to the nearest electricity outlet; unless your local council has installed charging points at parking lots and other public spaces – as far as I know they're not too keen to do that. However, I'm ideal for getting around and about in town. You'd never cover more than 100 miles a day driving in a town, which means you can plug me into your wall socket in the evening when we get back home, and leave me to recharge overnight. If you have solar panels or a wind generator on your roof, you could recharge me for free.

I'm supposed to be a 'green' car, but I won't truly become one until people shut down their coal plants, natural gas incinerators and hydro power stations. Keeping things as they are will make the cities a bit cleaner, of course, because I don't produce any tailpipe emissions, but it will also mean building more coal plants and increasing the output of the existing ones, generating more pollution, contributing to deforestation ... Keeping things as they are is never good enough – we need change, don't you think?

Having said all that, experts claim that, apart from more-than-obvious pros, I have some really nasty cons. You'll be able to read about them later in this book, as I open my hood and let you have an exclusive preview of what I'm really made of.

one

Electric cars under scrutiny – facts & figures

The power of words

Before we delve into the amazing world of electric cars, I'd like to outline the terminology that I'll be using in this book:

Electric car – a road-going automobile that is directly powered by an electric motor.

Plug-in hybrid – a car that features at least two propulsion systems, one of which is an electric motor powered from a source of electricity (a battery) that can be recharged by plugging the car into a wall socket.

V – voltage; the electrical force that drives an electric current between two points. In Britain, home outlets have a voltage of 230V. In the USA, the majority of outlets will have 110V.

A – amperes; a measure of the amount of electric charge passing a certain point per second. In layman's terms it is the amount of current that flows through a wire. The most widespread rating in Britain is 13A. Though the grid is capable of more, it would be unsafe to provide households with a higher rating.

W – watt; a derived unit that measures the rate of energy conversion, i.e. how much work the electricity does. Subsequently, kW stands for a kilowatt (one thousand watts). According to Ohm's law, the amount of energy we can get out of our wall sockets is W = A x V, which, in Britain, is 13 x 230 = 2990W = 2.99kW.

kWh – kilowatt-hour; how much power you get from electricity in one hour. In ideal circumstances, where there's no energy loss, the 2.99kW from your wall socket will produce 2.99kWh.

AC/DC – one of the world's most influential rock bands ... oh, sorry, I got carried away. The current flowing through a wire is, in fact, a bunch of electrons moving from one point to another. If the electrons flow straight, we talk about direct current or DC. If the electrons follow an alternating

A typical older electric car – weird and cute. This one's an experimental model by Nissan, conceived in 1947. (Courtesy Nissan Motors)

route, it is alternating current or AC. Our wall sockets operate on AC, which is preferable because AC can carry more energy and travel further without losing too much energy. Likewise, an AC motor is more efficient than a DC one. That's why the majority of electric cars will use an AC motor. AC systems are more expensive than DC ones, hence the majority of personal DIY electric car conversions feature a DC motor.

NEV – neighbourhood electric vehicle; aka 'eggshell car.' A small and basic single- or two-seater vehicle with limited maximum speed (30mph usually) that can be driven on public roads where the speed restriction permits; meaning that it cannot be driven on roads where max speed limit is, for instance, 50mph. Outlawed in Canada due to safety flaws, NEVs are popular in the USA and (recently) in Britain. They are usually classified as heavy quad-bikes to eschew obligations of undergoing crash tests.

ZEV – zero emissions vehicles. A term coined by manufacturers who want to sell more electric cars. Although electric cars fall within the classification of ZEVs because they don't produce any tailpipe emissions, there are no true ZEVs available anywhere in the world, because the electricity the car would consume is coming from power plants that do emit, among other nasties, CO_2.

The main parts of an electric car
Electric motor The heart of the electric car. The motor converts electrical power into mechanical power. It is a very simple device with only two main parts – a stator and a rotor.

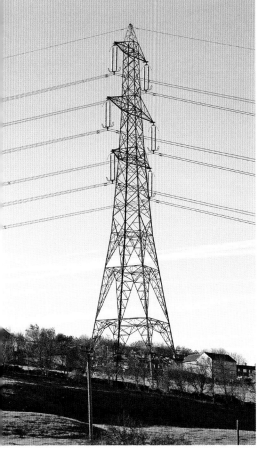

Britain is okay, but in some countries more electricity will have to be generated in order to support the demand for electric cars. (Courtesy Tim Green via Creative Commons Licence)

An electric motor in all its glory. (Courtesy PI Marketing Limited (UK))

Motor controller A computerized device that monitors the motor's speed, power consumption, and temperature. The signals from the 'throttle' pedal are sent to the controller, which then determines how much direct current should be taken from the batteries, converted to alternating current, and used to drive the motor.

Transmission Wait a little, does it need a transmission? Not necessarily. There are companies out there that are busying themselves with developing small-size gearboxes especially for electric cars but, in my opinion, they're wasting their time. All an electric car needs is a single reduction gear. It's unwise to connect a high-rev electric motor directly to the wheels, so the reduction gear will work as a mediator between the motor and the wheels. The reduction gear ratio in modern electric cars is anywhere between 5:1 to 10:1. For example, a reduction gear of 10:1

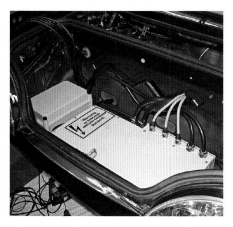

Motor controller – the brain of your electric car. (Courtesy PI Marketing Limited (UK))

means that for every ten revolutions a motor performs, the wheels will make just one revolution. The best thing about all this is that you don't need to shift gears any more. Direct current (DC) motor-powered cars will need a

Battery pack in an electric car conversion.
(Courtesy PI Marketing Limited (UK))

primitive gearbox that allows them to shift in reverse, but as the use of DC is gradually being phased out, being replaced by more efficient alternating current (AC) motors, no reverse gear will be necessary, because you can tell an AC motor to go in reverse by just hitting a button.

Batteries Just like your MP3 player, an electric car needs a rechargeable battery. Unlike your MP3 player, electric cars' batteries weigh hundreds of pounds. It is quite easy to comprehend the amount of energy storage that goes under the floor. The most basic battery used to power electric cars is a lead-acid battery; similar to the battery of a conventional car. Heavy and inefficient, one kilogram of lead-acid powerpack is capable of producing 0.025kWh of energy. Nickel metal hydride (NiMH) batteries give four times more energy from the same weight. So, the energy/weigh ratio of a NiMH battery is 0.1kWh per kg. Currently, the most advanced is the Lithium ion (Li-ion) battery, with as much as 0.16kWh per kg. If we assume that an average electric car consumes 0.25kWh per mile we will need to carry approximately 1.6kg of battery weight to cover each mile. A battery that can provide enough energy for a 100-mile travel range will weigh at least 160kg, not counting the safety equipment that goes with the battery pack.

The accompanying drawing

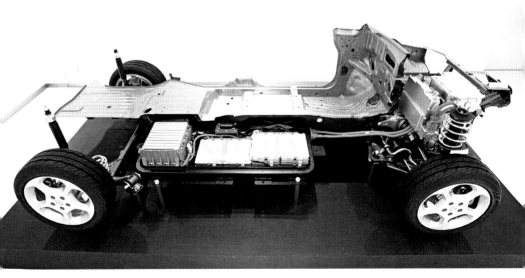

A marvellous image showing exactly how Li-ion battery packs fit under the floor of an electric car.
(Courtesy Nissan Motors)

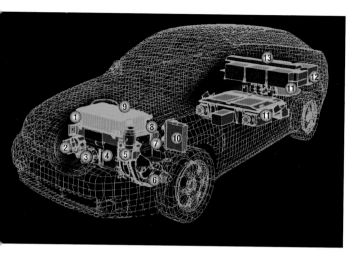

This drawing shows the basic layout of components in an electric car. Please see the text for explanation. (Courtesy Ford and Magna)

10. Vehicle control unit – the brain. This monitors and controls everything, from regenerative braking to power distribution between the driving wheels.

11. Battery pack; this is were the electricity comes from. The amount of battery cells depicted contains 23kWh of energy, which is good for covering roughly 100 miles between recharges.

12. AC charger. The battery needs DC (direct current), but you'll be plugging your car into an AC outlet. The charger's task is to convert AC to DC.

13. DC to DC converter. Many of the car's systems will need the usual 12V source (like the 12 volts produced by the lead-acid battery of a conventional car). This converter supplies electricity to a single 12V battery, which is used to power headlamps and other ancillary devices.

(provided by Ford and Magna) shows the basic layout of components in a front-wheel-drive electric car. The components can change from model to model, and not everything from this list is obligatory for a very basic electric car. A more advanced car, for example, will have more components than those listed.

1. Motor controller.
2. Air conditioning system.
3. Electric water pump that circulates the coolant necessary to take out whatever little heat there is in the electric motor and batteries. There's not a lot to cool, though.
4. Electric motor.
5. Power steering mechanism.
6. Transmission. In Ford's case it is a single speed reduction gear with a 5.4:1 reduction ratio.
7. A modular powertrain cradle fixes the motor to the chassis and provides anti-vibration insulation.
8. An electric vacuum pump powers the brake system and power steering.
9. A high voltage electric heater. This device heats the interior and helps control the battery temperature.

Electric car layouts

Just like a conventional car, there can be rear-wheel-drive, front-wheel-drive, and potentially, full-wheel-drive electric cars. It really doesn't make a lot of difference because at the speeds and distances involved, you probably won't notice.

Lunar Rover, the car that accompanied man to the moon, was a full-wheel-drive electric car, with a separate motor inside every wheel. This is actually quite an old idea. The German whizz-kid engineer Ferdinand Porsche created a full-wheel-drive electro-hybrid car when he was 25 years old. The light lorry was built when Porsche worked for Austrian motor plant Lohner, and the prototype, named Le Toujours Contente (Forever Satisfied), was shown to the public in 1901. Each wheel had a separate electric motor – or hub motor – that took power from a petrol engine that generated electricity.

Today, many companies are looking to bring Porsche's invention to a new level. In-wheel motors are regarded by many as the best way forward for full-wheel-drive electric cars. British company Protean Electric, for example, has a great deal of know-how in this rather obscure field.

It's possible to make a full-wheel-drive electric car in the conventional way, but it would require a more sophisticated transmission, and the power loss would be significant.

Efficiency of electric motors

With an internal combustion engine, only one quarter of a cycle generates power; the remaining three quarters are wasted. In the intake stroke the piston travels down and sucks the fuel mixture into the combustion chamber. During the compression stroke the piston travels upwards and pressurizes the fuel mixture. Half the cycle is complete but no power is produced as yet. Then boom, the fuel mixture explodes and sends the piston down; at last we get some power. During the exhaust stroke the piston travels up again. Meanwhile, two revolutions of the crankshaft have occurred, losing power due to friction, and producing waste heat.

With an electric motor, each and every millimeter of movement is used to generate power. An electric motor is as simple as a device can be. It is basically a stator (a shell) and a rotor that rotates within the stator. Nothing is wasted – a rotor makes power and

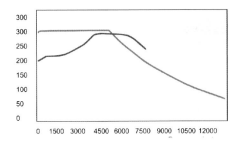

Follow the green line! An electric motor generates a constant value of torque up until 5000rpm. Compare it with an internal combustion engine. This particular graph is based on information provided by Tesla Motors; other modern AC electric motors will not vary significantly.

torque throughout every part of every revolution. A modern AC motor is so small and light that you can easily put it inside a small travel suitcase and carry it away. And electric motors produce almost no waste heat. This is both good and bad, though. Good because we don't like to waste power, and bad because we get cold and grumpy. With an internal combustion engine you get so much waste heat that you can achieve a comforting warmth inside the car. When driving an electric car, however, it is a challenge to keep the interior warm. Check the Pros & Cons chapter for more on this problem and for a possible solution.

When it comes to generating electricity, the first words that spring to mind are 'inefficiency' and 'waste.' The power plants that involve heat and turbines will convert approximately only 30 per cent of the input into electricity. With wind generators, it's hard to calculate the efficiency, but, as a matter of fact, they will stay idle for 65 to 80 per cent of their lifetime. After considering the 'leakages' that happen before the power actually hits your wheels, more than three quarters of the valuable energy is lost. It is barely better than an average internal combustion engine that still works with some 20 per cent efficiency – not a big change since the 1920s, I must say.

In 2009 in the UK around 28,000gWh of electricity was lost in transition. That's more than seven per cent of the total yearly production. The motor in your electric car is indeed very efficient. It converts around 80 per cent of input energy into mechanical movement. There's not much friction going on, it doesn't need to comprise over a hundred moving parts (in contrast to the internal combustion engine), it doesn't generate a lot of waste heat – that's why it needs an auxiliary heating system if you're not lucky enough to have been born close to the equator. Basically, it is the way we generate electricity that makes electric cars relatively inefficient at the moment.

What makes an electric car cheaper to use and potentially better for the environment is the fact that it takes less power to drive than a similar petrol car. In other words, it is more efficient. We already discovered that an electric car can do four miles on one kWh (on average 0.25kWh per mile). The average petrol car doing 23mpg will demand a whopping 1.58kWh per mile. A hybrid car is rather significantly better by consuming as little as 0.52kWh per mile in a mixed cycle (considering its low-speed propulsion is supplied by the electric motor, and the regenerative braking system works). This calculation takes into account that petrol can generate 9.6kWh per litre. It is the most accurate calculation for comparing two hardly comparable things – electric motors and internal combustion engines. Although theoretically the efficiency of an electric motor is 80 per cent, in the real world it is very far from it because the electricity is generated in

an inefficient way. If, for example, there are two similar fossil fuel engines, both 20 per cent efficient, one powering a car and the other generating electricity for an electric car, the electric car will be only 16 per cent efficient.

Regenerative braking

In overrun (when braking or rolling down a hill) the electric motor acts as a generator developing electricity that is fed back into the battery. Otherwise, this valuable kinetic energy would be wasted.

Unlike a petrol car, the majority of electric cars will have a longer range in the city than outside the city. With a petrol car you're consuming much more fuel in the urban cycle than when you're just cruising down a freeway at a constant speed. Thanks to regenerative braking, and the fact that near-maximum power and torque is achieved even at very low revs, an electric car will last longer in the urban driving cycle than when going near its maximum speed. This is another reason why an electric car is almost perfect for city driving.

Electric cars and cold weather

It seems that global warming has brought us some of the coldest winters of recent years, though, of course, across the majority of Europe and North America cold winters are common. Although you might be looking forward to all those wintry delights like building snowmen and rolling in the snow, your electric car certainly is not. If a conventional car takes energy for heating the interior from the waste heat that is produced by the good old low-efficiency internal combustion engine, but there is almost no waste heat produced by an electric motor. Hence, if you want to have some sort of interior heating, the energy will have to

The motor turns the wheel

Braking: the wheel turns the motor

Regenerative braking. Top illustration: the motor takes power from a battery and turns the wheel. Bottom illustration: you start braking, the motor stops powering the wheel. Instead, it becomes a generator; the wheel continues to turn the motor until the car has come to a halt; electricity is safely deposited back into the battery.

come out of the battery. To make things even gloomier, the winter will take out another ten to 20 per cent of battery capacity due to peculiarities of chemical processes that produce the current. Thus, each time the temperature draws closer to zero, the range of an electric car will fall by almost a third.

But there might be a solution. Again, it's not something that we can just take and plonk onto a car. It needs more research and tweaking but something is still better than nothing. Do you remember I said "almost no waste heat." There are moving parts in an electric motor and where there's movement, there's friction and heat.

Audi has developed a mobile heat pump for electric cars. Until now a heat pump was something that posh people used to heat their mansions. A rather expensive and sophisticated device that takes scarce heat from beneath the earth's surface and through a clever thermodynamic intervention 'pumps up' the heat to a temperature that is usable for heating.

The Audi e-tron prototype shown at the Detroit Car Show demonstrated a small heat pump that would, to a certain extent, solve the problem with heating. Many parts of Germany are covered in snow during the winter and if Audi is to stand any chance of having an edge over its competitors it had to come up with something revolutionary. It's hard to 'warm up' to the idea of using a heat pump in a car, mostly due to the fact that we associate heat pumps with devices that take up the best part of our basement space.

But wait, is there a catch? Ah! I believe there is. A heat pump still consumes electricity to carry out all that thermodynamic abracadabra; and electricity will be taken from the batteries. However, estimates suggest that a car equipped with a heat pump will save a certain amount of energy compared to a car that feeds electricity directly into convectors.

Kewet Buddies dodge the harsh Scandinavian winter, and prove that electric cars and cold weather can go together pretty well. (Courtesy Elbil Norge)

two

Electric cars & money

How much does it cost to run an electric car?

It's actually relatively cheap. A modern AC motor will consume 0.25kWh of energy per mile. That's not much if you compare it with any domestic appliance. For example, a 100W light bulb will use 0.1kWh. A DC motor will be less efficient, consuming around 0.4kWh per mile. How does this compare with a conventional car? Well, the maths is pretty simple here. I'll spare you the tedious mega joules and thermodynamics formulae, and just look at a simple thing like distance. While driving a car it's all we care about – how far will this car get me on one fuel tank, sorry, charge. It largely depends on where you live and what energy supplier you use, but there are trends. I like watching trends and I'll use them to tell you how much you could save by switching to electricity.

In the UK the average retail price for electricity is £0.10 per kWh (16.5c)

whereas in the USA it's £0.07 ($0.12). A kWh can get you a long way. In fact, although you always get grumpy when you receive your electricity bill, we must consider ourselves lucky, as the price of electricity is very friendly at the moment. Unfortunately, that's mainly due to the fact that we are still relying too much on cheap coal-generated power (more on that later) and that there is an oil price war going on in the world. I think you've noticed. We're paying much more for fuel than it is actually worth.

OK, no more politics, I promise (well, at least for a couple of pages). So, our electric car will cost £0.025 ($0.041) per mile to drive considering that an AC motor allows us to drive four miles with every kWh. It is cheaper to drive an electric car in the USA – £1.75 ($0.03) per mile. In comparison, to hit the throttle on a 'normal' car, you'd now need around £0.17 ($0.28) per mile in the UK and £0.06 ($0.10) in the USA. So, switching to electricity could

Cost per mile	Electric car	Petrol car	Savings
UK	£0.025 ($0.041)	£0.17 ($0.28)	85 per cent
USA	£1.75 ($0.03)	£0.06 ($0.10)	70 per cent

give you a whopping 70 to 85 per cent saving. It's not fair that fuel is so cheap in America, I'm turning green with envy, but on the other hand it is not bad to have better savings in the UK.

However, the table above depicts the ideal world. In the real world, you may have to have to account for the batteries. Some electric cars that go on sale in 2011 will be supplied with a 'batteries not included' clause. You'll get your battery pack on a lease contract costing around $100 per month. Now, if you're driving less than 1000 miles per month, the electric car becomes less viable. With other, more expensive, electric cars you'll get to own the batteries, but considering that no-one dares to predict the actual lifespan of batteries, there might be a possibility that you'd have to replace the whole battery pack in five years (mileage around 50,000). A new battery pack would cost more than the value of your then-used electric car. However, if you opted for extending the life of your car by spending £3000 on a new battery pack, you'd have to consider that each mile you cover cost you an extra six pence (3000 divided by 50,000). The same calculation applies to all DIY electric car conversions (read more in the Conversion chapter) when you need to factor in the price of the battery pack. OK, even if we add £0.06 to the £0.025 from the table, it is £0.085, which is exactly half the running cost of a petrol car. Not bad, eh?

There is an alternative way to compare the energy consumption of electric cars and petrol cars. Crystallized after an almost 20-year long argument,

the US Department of Energy has come up with a following procedure.

"The petroleum-equivalent fuel economy for an electric vehicle is calculated as follows:
1. Determine the electric vehicle's Urban Dynamometer Driving Schedule energy consumption value and the Highway Fuel Economy Driving Schedule energy consumption value in units of watt-hours per mile;
2. Determine the combined energy consumption value by averaging the Urban Dynamometer Driving Schedule energy consumption value and the Highway Fuel Economy Driving Schedule energy consumption value using a weighting of 55 percent urban/45 percent highway;
3. Calculate the petroleum-equivalent fuel economy by dividing the appropriate petroleum-equivalency factor (depending on whether any petroleum-powered accessories are installed; by the combined energy consumption value, and round to the nearest 0.01 miles per gallon.

The petroleum-equivalency factors for electric vehicles are as follows:
1. If the electric vehicle does not have any petroleum-powered accessories installed, the value of the petroleum equivalency factor is 82,049 watt-hours per gallon.
2. If the electric vehicle has any petroleum-powered accessories installed, the value of the petroleum equivalency factor is 73,844 watt-hours per gallon."

Wow! That's really worth 20 years. OK, to cut a long story short: according to the US Department of Energy an average electric car capable of 0.25kWh per mile consumption would be equivalent to a petrol car that does 162mpg (that's UK Imperial gallons – 1.74 litres per 100km for continental Europe). The production car with an internal combustion engine to even come close this level is the Volkswagen Lupo 1.2-litre diesel that consumes three litres of diesel fuel on 100km (94mpg).

Volkswagen built a one-litre per 100km diesel car. Called the 1L, it was not a production car – more of an experiment to prove the efficiency of diesel engines. The VW concept really did manage one-litre per 100km (282mpg) and it's an amazing achievement. Although 1L is a roadworthy car, there are certain reasons why it is so economical. Its body drag coefficient is only 0.159 (0.26 to 0.33 in production cars) and it is a very light vehicle, weighing only 290kg. To make the experiment valid, VW constructed the car with all the necessary safety features, like crunch zones and roll-over protection. However, it would be mighty expensive if was produced in series. It just shows the potential of diesel.

Actual fuel consumption and operating cost are the best factors on which to compare different means of transportation. We can also look at the amount of energy carried by electricity and fossil fuel, we can take a whole bunch of clever scientific terms and turn this book into a guide for geeks. However, in the end it will be the retail price of electric cars that decides who wins – electricity or internal combustion. Another good way of comparing alternative energy cars with the conventional internal combustion vehicles is to look at how big an impact they have on our environment. Please read the Blackouts, Prices,

Lupo 1L undergoes a real-life test on a German autobahn. Several VW vans are providing an escort and monitoring the data.
(Courtesy VolksWagen)

Powerstations section for more insights to ecology.

A major issue in switching to electric cars will be that people start comparing them with petrol cars on an emotional level. If you buy an electric car now, you will probably be downgrading and downsizing from your current level of comfort and equipment. Driving an electric car feels different, it requires developing new habits, and you always get less car for your money. £19,000 will buy a 4.8 metre family Ford Mondeo petrol car, or a small, three metre electric car. The question you need to ask yourself is – do I need a five-seater, and, if I buy it, how often will the rear seats be occupied? If you're only driving around town, and mainly on your own, it's very likely you don't need a petrol car. If, however, you regularly do longer distances, you might struggle with an electric car, but you still can consider a plug-in hybrid.

Little perks for going green

In 2009 the British government announced that it would splash out £250 million to give electric cars a head start. £20 million would go towards introducing a charging infrastructure for electric cars (in addition to £13 million secured by the Conservative Mayor of London Boris Johnson from private investors and Transport for London). At the time of writing there are more than 200 charging points in London, but Mr Johnson wants to build another 7500 to support his dream of 100,000 electric cars in London by 2020. The Labour party in turn wanted to encourage people out of their cars. There's nothing wrong with wanting, the only thing is that it will never happen. People and cars is an eternal love affair, so it would be more effective to encourage people into adopting greener habits (some tips are in the last chapter) than to encourage them out of their cars.

On January 1st, 2011, the UK government will unleash the remaining £230 million in the form of a subsidy for those who decide to buy an electric car or a plug-in hybrid. Some say this is rather controversial because the low speed (think eggshell, think not too safe) NEVs and conventional hybrid cars (the ones that cannot be plugged in and charged from an outlet) will not qualify for this tempting £5000 incentive. Many people are waiting for the New Year in trepidation. Looks like the only available proper electric cars on the market will be the Tesla Roadster and the Mitsubishi i MiEV. Both appealing to different kinds of buyers but having something very much in common – they are rather expensive! The quirky Lotus Elise-based Roadster has a base price of £86,000 in Britain, while the small family car i MiEV costs £25,000, which, for its size, is considered too high. Although one must appreciate that the Mitsubishi is a great package of high-tech ... what a lot of people are worried about is that affluent buyers will have the first go at claiming their discounts on the expensive electric cars. That, I must say is a little unfair.

The £230 million pot allows for a whopping 46,000 electric cars and plug-in hybrids to be subsidized. If the first part of 2011 sees a few hundred Roadsters and i MiEVs sold in Britain, I'd call it a very successful start. Those 46,000 allocations will last us well into 2012 even though the majority of people will be jumping into the smaller electric cars. So, don't worry, if you're really into electric cars, it's likely you'll have a chance to get your subsidy. The early part of 2011 should also see the long-awaited Nissan Leaf family car and the Norwegian Th!nk, which, although small, is highway capable and at the moment one of only two electric cars (the other being the Tesla Roadster) to have passed a proper crash test. It is very probable that the Toyota Prius Plug-in will make it in time for the subsidy with the on sale target set to the latter part of 2011. Although the range of just five cars to choose from might seem a little unattractive, however, considering the novelty of the electric car market, it is good that customers are getting five safe vehicles. The i MiEV will have no problem passing a crash test. According to the National Agency for Automotive Safety and Victim's Aid (Japan), the petrol version of the Mitsubishi i passed the rigorous Japanese crash tests rather brilliantly by getting five out of six stars. The recent Nissan model history suggests that the Nissan Leaf (a proper size family car) will also easily pass the crash tests.

The thing with grants and subsidies is that we, the taxpayers, are basically being taken for a ride, because it's our money that they're using for the electric car subsidies. It's not a complaint, though. We're still getting something back and that's not a bad thing at all.

Maybe the USA, where the incentive for buying green goods is tax relief rather than money, has taken a better approach. One question that has been asked, though, is how the US government plans to fill the gap in the budget. However, as there is no mass-scale craze for electric cars yet, it won't be too big a gap to fill.

In Britain, the £5000 subsidy is not the only incentive available. The Office for Low Emission Vehicles has more little perks in its candy jar. Electric cars are Congestion Charge exempt in London. You'll be able to enjoy the comfort of your own vehicle while driving through the heart of London without paying the dreaded charge. Free or reduced cost parking will be made available for E-car owners. This all makes London a great place to be driving electric. But what about the rest of the country? Commercial entities will love this – electrifying your fleet now means vehicle excise duty exemption, an enhanced capital allowance, and a lower rate of company car tax. This is especially appealing to delivery companies operating within the vehicle's range.

Even better if you're in business

If you're running a business, purchasing a green car makes more sense than ever. In Britain you will qualify for a 100 per cent first year capital allowance on certain types of low-emission vehicles that emit less than 110g/km CO_2 (177g/mile). Capital allowance means that you can deduct a proportion of certain purchases from your company's taxable profits, and reduce your tax bill by a tidy sum. Obviously, electric cars are classified within this low emission range because they are 'zero-emission' vehicles. Of course, they're not. I know, it's rather unfair because an electric car can potentially produce more than 177g/mile if it's powered from a provider that prevalently delivers coal-plant electricity. While the government hasn't acknowledged that, you can enjoy the tax

break. The rules will be reviewed in 2013, so if you're thinking about painting your fleet green, 2011 is the best time to start.

It's surprising how many businesses forget to claim capital allowance. So, considering your company's tax bill is a significant amount, even if you're looking at a relatively expensive electric car for your business, you don't have to worry about the price. Even the ridiculously-priced Mitsubishi iMiEV (£39,000) doesn't look much. And there is nothing that says you cannot use an iMiEV as a delivery vehicle. Just don't forget to look at the local electric car producers first. Buying locally is one of the best things you can do for the environment and the future job prospects of your children.

It might be difficult for a person or a family to switch to an entirely different way of motoring. For small and medium businesses, it might prove an easier task, especially if the business is based in a large town, and particularly if it has something to do with deliveries or despatches, etc. Think pizza delivery man – short, frequent runs within the city, and no work during the night so that the car can sit in a garage and take the charge.

Tax breaks in the US

Almost every person buying a new alternative energy vehicle is entitled to a significant tax break. There are different methods to calculate the benefit for hybrid vehicle owners, but where the plug-in electric cars are concerned there is a minimum tax break of $2500 on offer. There's a certain early-bird effect to this system because, once the manufacturer has sold 200,000 vehicles, the tax benefit will be reduced and gradually phased out. The limit on conventional hybrids is even lower – 60,000 cars sold. That's why the Toyota Prius doesn't qualify for tax relief in the

Congratulations to Ford, commiserations to the customers – the majority of Ford hybrids are not eligible for an incentive any more due to the large number of vehicles produced. (Courtesy Ford USA)

USA any more. In 2006 you could get a neat $3150 as a thank you for buying a Prius but the benefit amount went through the floor as the car advanced on the market, reaching zero by October 2007. At the time of writing, the most attractive tax credits for hybrid cars are on the Ford Fusion and the Mercury Mariner – $3400 and $3000 respectively. This situation already sees an increase in the popularity of home-made hybrid cars.

The maximum credit you can get buying an all-electric car in America is $7500. The amount of credit depends on the battery capacity. The longer the range, the more money back. Thus a proper electric car with a decent range costing $30,000 will lose a quarter off its price thanks to a tax rebate. To qualify, the purchased vehicle has to have at least four wheels. Yes! At last somebody is considering road safety and not automatically endorsing eggshell cars. Three-wheeled NEVs and electric bikes qualify only for a ten per cent purchase price tax break. The benefit system will be reviewed later in 2011, so it makes sense to use it while it is available. Tax benefits on conversion electric cars are always available – check the Conversion chapter for more information.

Different tax breaks and capital allowances are available in Europe, Canada, Mexico, and some other countries. Please check with your tax advisor or local business forums (many of them available online) before you purchase a vehicle.

Electric car insurance

For many car insurers electric cars are like the territory of the Wild West – full of unknown risks and dangers. Because the technology is so new, they don't really have a system to calculate the probability of something going wrong. And things will go wrong occasionally, only no-one really knows how much it would cost to repair an electric car. To a certain extent insurers base their premium calculations on statistics; and there is no data available on electric cars.

Talking about risks, firemen and rescue workers will need to undergo special training to recognize electric cars and make decisions accordingly. In emergency situations, for example, flooding and serious road accidents, they would have to approach the situation differently than if it was a disaster involving petrol cars only.

Although electric cars are relatively safe, electric shock and irritant fumes from batteries would need to be considered by the rescue workers.

So, electric car insurance is not a straightforward topic. Although Richard Turnbull from Electric Car Corporation told me that from the 150 ev'ie cars, they've sold in London, all have been insured with different companies on a hassle-free basis, the majority of price comparison websites won't be able to give you a full picture because they wouldn't recognize your car. Still, the good old method with a copy of Yellow Pages and a phone should do the trick, and at least some of the established companies will be relatively happy to insure an electric car.

three

Electric cars & the environment

The thing about electric cars – and many, many environmental activists get this wrong – is that an electric car is NOT a zero emission vehicle. Although no nasties come out of its exhaust (it doesn't even have one), it won't be zero emission unless you charge the batteries exclusively from wind, solar, or other type of green energy. Don't forget that in most cases fossil fuel is used to produce electricity. Your electric car is as green as the energy it consumes. See the pie charts for the electricity sources in the UK and USA. If you cannot find yourself on the green slice, you won't make the world a better place by driving an electric car. As you see, fossil fuels, such as coal and natural gas, still dominate electricity production.

The following table shows how many grams of CO_2 is released by generating one kilowatt-hour of electricity from different energy sources. As you can see, 1kWh of coal plant electricity costs the environment 874 grams of CO_2. If we assume that

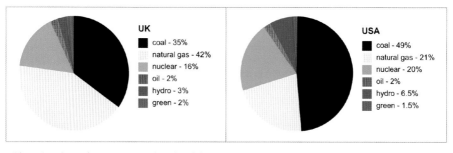

UK
- coal - 35%
- natural gas - 42%
- nuclear - 16%
- oil - 2%
- hydro - 3%
- green - 2%

USA
- coal - 49%
- natural gas - 21%
- nuclear - 20%
- oil - 2%
- hydro - 6.5%
- green - 1.5%

Your electric car is as green as the electricity that powers it. Where is your energy coming from?

Energy source	g per kWh	g per mile	*In most cases there
Coal	874	218.5	are no CO_2 emissions from
Natural gas	440	110	green sources, but things
Oil/petrol	800	200	like grey energy needed to
Hydro-electric	4	1	produce photovoltaics and
Nuclear	6	1.5	lubricant needed to oil the
Green electricity*	32	8	giant wind turbines should
			be taken into account.

the average electric car takes 0.25kWh of electricity to cover a mile, it would indirectly emit 218g CO_2 per mile should you have recharged it from a coal plant. The data in this table is compiled using two statistical sources provided by ADEME (French Environment and Energy Management Agency) and Oak Ridge National Laboratory (Tennessee, USA) to account for regional variations of fossil fuels.

Therefore, if your energy supplier used only coal to produce energy, your 'zero emission' electric car would emit 218g CO_2 per mile, which is more than a 'normal' car emits. The average for a modern petrol car is in the region of 200-220g per mile, while a 1.6-litre diesel is capable of 160g per mile.

It is very rare, though, that electricity coming out of your wall socket is 100 per cent coal-generated. Most energy suppliers will diversify their energy sources. Let's go back to those pie charts and do some calculations. Imagine an energy supplier whose energy portfolio is proportioned in accordance to the country pie charts, i.e. 35 per cent of electricity would be bought from coal plants, 41 per cent from natural gas incinerators, and so on. We can roughly conclude that electric cars generate 124.2g CO_2 per mile in Britain, and 134.5g in the USA.

A pretty decent result but nothing to brag about. That is a little bit less than a petrol car but as it is technically possible to build a petrol car that produces only 100g CO_2 per mile, consider an electric car as a motoring alternative and a way to save money, not as green transport at the very moment. Because there's no way of knowing where your electricity really comes from. The fact that your country's average is 35 per cent of electricity generated from coal, doesn't mean that your personal energy supplier follows this proportion. It might well be more than 35 per cent, or there might be some imported energy coming down the wire, making it even less environmentally friendly.

To be perfectly correct, we should readjust our calculation by introducing a life-cycle assessment of some sort. The easiest one to use is the concept of well-to-wheel. It includes two stages: well-to-tank (w-t-t) and tank-to-wheel (t-t-w). The w-t-t shows how much energy it takes to generate the fuel. In the case of a petrol car, we have to consider that oil is being pumped out of the earth, refined and transported to the petrol station. The t-t-w is the efficiency of the fuel once it has ended up in your car's fuel tank. According to the US Department of Energy the current well-to-tank efficiency of a petrol car is 83 per cent. So, when I mentioned that a modern petrol car would emit 220g of CO_2 per mile, I should have factored in the w-t-t efficiency and conclude that the real amount of emissions is 265g per mile.

The table that shows emissions per

energy source for the electric cars also refers to the well-to-tank (from the power station to your socket). Unfortunately, we cannot use the whole of each kWh we get out of the wall socket. According to Tesla Motors (Martin Eberhard's and Marc Tarpenning's study for the Stanford University, 2006), electric cars lose 14 per cent of electricity through the charging process. You put 1kWh of charge into the battery but you get out only 0.86kWh. Neil Hutchinson, who converted his MG cabrio to run with electricity, told me that charging is 92 per cent efficient. As this is almost exactly the number I've got from other independent sources, I'll stick with 92. Thus, the real amount of carbon emissions if coal electricity is used will be 236g per mile, and, with combined-source electricity, 135g per mile (UK) and 146.2g per mile (USA). Look! We've found another 11 per cent in favour of the electric car!

The next table, below, indicates how much coal some countries use to generate electricity. France and Norway are well ahead of others. Also, Finland and Spain currently have the highest

Country	Coal, per cent	Green energy, per cent
Australia	76	1.5
Canada	18	2
China	81	near 0
Finland	27	13
France	5	2
Germany	48	11.5
Great Britain	35	5
Japan	27	2.5
Norway	0.1	1
Russia	16.5	near 0
Spain	25	11
South Africa	94	near 0
USA	49	3

proportion of green electricity. The data comes from the International Energy Agency (IEA) and is correct for the beginning of 2008 when the last report was published. The situation might have changed a little but don't expect a hugely improved picture. Actually, some countries, contrary to our expectations, have increased the output of their coal plants since 2008.

The way we consume coal is totally dreadful. 30 years ago the world consumed 2115 megatons of coal every year to generate electricity, heat, etc. Today, we're consuming 4580 megatons. That's a 216 per cent increase.

Considering that currently nearly 95 per cent of the world's electricity is generated through non-sustainable sources, you might be doing the right thing by driving a car with a small diesel engine. The efficiency of a modern diesel engine can be up to 50 per cent (compare to 20-30 per cent of a petrol engine), which is amazing for a thermodynamic engine. I'm not saying that there's no potential in the future for electric cars. Even now, if you're confident about the source of your electricity, you might be cutting pollution and CO_2 emissions by switching to an electric car today. For more coal facts, please go to the 'Real Environmental Issues' chapter.

Blackouts, prices, powerstations

The main reason why an electric car seems so attractive is its relatively low running costs. Honestly, the only reason why we're talking about electric cars at all might be that people cannot afford to pay for fuel. It's not just the Third World that has trouble 'cookin' with gas' – the richest countries of the world have a striking rate of fuel poverty as well. For example, in the UK, an estimated 4.5 million households (that's 17 per cent) are finding it difficult to foot their fuel bills. This is according to a study carried out by Energywatch, the consumer organisation looking after the interests of gas and electricity consumers in the UK. The general assumption is that the figure could be higher because not everyone is admitting to having problems. Even the middle class now struggles to pay for fuel and natural gas. The only relatively affordable source of energy is electricity, and that's likely to remain the case for at least a decade ... or, as some experts suggest, electricity might even fall in price as we learn to harness various sources of renewable energy, and some of us even leave our energy providers for good to start a new life off the grid.

Those of us who are homeowners have the potential to generate our own electricity via solar batteries on the roof, and miniature private wind generators. See how flexible electricity is? You couldn't possibly source your own oil or natural gas even if you happened to live above an oil well. In reality, 'they' would just relocate you, no questions asked.

Everyone can build their own little 'rooftop power station' with relatively little outlay (in the low thousands of pounds).

In the UK in some cases no planning permission is required to fix solar panels on a roof of a single-dwelling house. For apartment blocks, listed buildings, and other cases, planning permission will be necessary. In most cases you would need to apply for planning permission from your local authority to add a domestic wind turbine to your house or grounds surrounding your home. Wind turbines that are attached to the roof or the wall also must comply with house building regulations. If the electrical installation of a solar panel or wind turbine doesn't come as a plug-in kit, you will need a certified electrician to come and do the wiring for you. Please read further

about the feed-in tariffs before you do anything.

In reality, electricity has the potential to fall in price. In a sense, we are regulating the price of this commodity via our own habits. A decrease in demand would also mean that prices go down.

Many people are worried that with the advance of electric cars we will all be faced with blackouts, candle-lit suppers, and groping around in the darkness. Although energy shortage is highly probable in some parts of the world, there's no immediate danger during the first stages of the electric car launch. That said, it's essential that we have a decent long-term strategy for generating more green electricity. That strategy would have to be pretty groundbreaking in order to be able to sustain a really large fleet of electric cars.

According to the International Energy Agency, in 2007 the UK produced 3400GWh of excess energy, which was then exported. If we consider that an average electric car consumes 0.25kWh per mile, and runs roughly 10,000 miles per year, the exported amount is enough to power more than a million electric cars. As our energy consumption falls each year due to more diligent use and better home appliances, it is quite possible that we can squeeze out another few megawatts of excess electricity for our electric cars. So, if we can believe the statistics, neither the UK nor the USA would have problems in supporting the initial surge of electric cars. Some European countries, like Italy, Ireland and Portugal, though, where a significant amount of electricity is imported, might be less lucky.

Also, it's wrong to calculate just the electricity consumed by electric cars on the road. We mustn't forget that establishing and running the new factories and infrastructure will end up being a huge burden on our grid.

On a worldwide scale, it's clear that by consuming more electricity we will have to produce more. How?

Building more coal plants is simply not an option (read the chapter about the environmental issues to learn more). One can hope that at least the civilized part of the world will understand that. What other weapons have we in our arsenal? Increasing the fleet of electric cars will inevitably mean an increase in electricity consumption. Wind farms are very unlikely to make much difference (and I'll discuss why later), which leaves us with ... what? More nuclear power stations? Personally, if I had to choose between a coal plant and a nuke, I would always go for nuke.

In the UK we consume roughly 400,000GWh of electricity. The target is to reach 15 per cent of energy produced using sustainable resources by 2015. And we all know how difficult it'll be to achieve those targets, especially when it comes to environmental stuff. Bureaucracy and lack of vision always interfere. France, for example, had a target to produce at least 36,000GWh of wind energy by 2010. We can all see that they are nowhere near the target, having produced only about 6000GWh of wind energy in 2009. I'm not saying this to haul France over the coals. It's just that those targets always tend to get the better of you no matter how determined you are. Realistically speaking, we won't probably achieve 15 per cent sustainable energy by 2015.

Wind power is often hailed the 'best way forward' to our green future. One can see why – in 2000 Cristina Archer and Mark Jacobson from Stanford University in sunny California finished a fascinating scientific paper explaining the benefits of wind power. They had painstakingly gathered data about average wind speeds around the world. The wind speed had been measured at an 80-metre elevation (that's how high the average wind turbine is) and where no measurements were available, they estimated the speed using extrapolation. They found that only 13 per cent of the planet's surface is suitable for wind power generation, i.e. wind speeds are at least 6.9m/s. If we place at least six 1500kW wind turbines on that 13 per cent surface, the amount of electricity generated will be five times more than the world currently consumes. So, you see, wind power has a huge potential. So, why don't we use it?

Let's try to dissect what is to become one of the largest wind farms in Europe. According to information provided by the energy supplier E-on, the Anglo-Danish project codenamed London Array plans to build 270 gigantic (120-metre rotors) wind generators 13 miles off the coast in the Thames estuary. The total output of the windfarm would reach 1000MW, which translates as approximately 2400GWh of electricity or at least 240,000 British households off the grid. The output of the new windfarm equals 0.6 per cent of what we consume each year. If that costs two billion Euros to build, the set target of 15 per cent would

Are they looking good? I don't know, but they're good for the environment!
(Courtesy Micah Maziar, released via Creative Commons Licence)

take 50 billion. If you like to play with hypothetical numbers, you can calculate that to wind-power the whole of the UK it would take 0.333 trillion Euros, and to take the entirety of Europe off the grid – seven trillion Euros. And then nobody speaks about how much CO_2 would be generated to produce thousands of wind generators and thousands of miles of underwater cables. Nobody speaks about it because nobody can give an estimate, and besides it's too inconvenient to discuss.

So, going back to the calculation carried out by Stanford University, we would need to build 550,000 gigantic 120-metre generators around the world to meet the total electricity demands (the world needs a power output of 2TW – equivalent of 16,830,000GWh). It means more than 2000 windfarms like the London Array. However, not every country can afford those 3.6MW generators. If the more conventional and traditional 1.5MW generators are used, we need more than 1.3 million of those. Sounds like mission impossible, but you cannot discount the fact that somebody built the pyramids ... and then there's Stonehenge.

The conclusion to all this is that we need a so-called portfolio approach to green energy – developing and integrating various different alternative energy resources.

Other green motoring options
The electric car is not the only way towards a green motoring future. As we discovered earlier, the world needs to adapt the portfolio approach by developing several different sustainable technologies. It is more than certain that one element of this sustainable development will deal with making conventional petrol vehicles more efficient.

Some of us may recall the weird-looking Wartburg import from Eastern Germany. It was sold in the UK during the

late '60s and early '70s. It had a three-cylinder two-stroke engine, with power around 50bhp, and capable of up to 50mpg. Its only purpose was to get you from A to B – nothing funky and nothing unnecessary. Many proper size family cars well into the '80s and '90s had 40bhp engines and no-one really seemed to mind. If you are an honest driver and you don't fancy breaking the law, in 99 per cent of cases you won't need a car that does more than 100mph and accelerates to 60mph faster than in ten seconds. There are simply not enough places in the UK (and I believe in most other countries) where you can safely and legally go over 100mph or accelerate to 60mph in two seconds. You're not exactly going to take your car to Silverstone every weekend to give it a good hammering. It's all about status. Who's got the most horses to boast about while having a pint of beer with mates? Reducing the average engine size and power wouldn't affect the quality of everyday motoring.

America tends to agree with this unpopular stance. In mid 2009, the government handed out an $8-billion low interest loan towards developing greener means of motoring.

Your new petrol car is only a little more efficient than than this lovable 1950s Austin A30. Another question – is it as cute? (Courtesy Michael G Spiller via Creative Commons Licence)

Unexpectedly, almost three thirds of the hunky sum was assigned to the traditional car makers so that they could make their gas-guzzlers guzzle less. It is perhaps quite a wise strategy. There is a huge room for improvement when it comes to petrol cars. They haven't really improved much since WWII because they didn't have to.

Obviously, the cheapest and easiest way to increase the mpg of any given car is to reduce its engine size and cut the power (to a sensible level, so that it optimally fits its body and purpose). But there are many other things you can do with an internal combustion engine to improve its efficiency. Electronic augmentation of combustion and gas exchange is one way. The theoretical efficiency of the Otto cycle (the set of thermodynamics laws that are executed inside the engine) is around 60 per cent. An engine of a street car is 20-25 per cent efficient. We are very far from making the most of the internal combustion engine and, although in the real world it is not possible to achieve a 60 per cent efficiency (60 per cent of the energy generated is converted into motion), we can always try to claw back the odd per cent or two from the unforgiving world of theoretical physics.

Heat convertors

The majority of the energy that comes out of the internal combustion engine is heat. If we could convert at least a small part of that waste heat into motion, that would be really good! Thermocoupling is a method that seldom gets mentioned in connection with cars, yet it is a very good, little known method of generating electricity from heat. If you plait two different metal wires (copper and iron, for example) together and start heating one end of the braid, you'll clock a meagre current at the other end. My compatriot Thomas Johann Seebeck

discovered this effect in 1821. If a hybrid car's petrol engine had an outer layer incorporating thermocouples, it would generate free electricity on the go and deposit it back into the battery or feed directly to the electric motor. Many other heat-converting technologies are available that could be adapted for use in hybrid cars. I am sure somebody will come to that conclusion eventually.

Driving a used car

This is one of the easiest and cheapest short-term solutions of green motoring. It is not something that would fit everyone, though. For example, I've never liked, wanted or needed a new car and I've always driven used diesels (because diesels are more efficient than petrol engines). With a little bit of DIY and regular repairs, an old car can serve well for good few years. The greenness of this approach is cutting the grey energy that goes into producing a new car. The whole manufacturing process of a new internal combustion car accounts for 15,000kg (equivalent of 35,000kWh) CO_2 emissions. A new electric car would cause a similar amount of manufacturing emissions;

They say you can find a real gem in a second-hand car lot like this. The front one is cute, but you can tell from the expression on its face that it's a gas-guzzler. Let's go further and look for a good-quality diesel.
(Courtesy John Lloyd via Creative Commons Licence)

maybe even more because battery production is very carbon-intensive. So, when you leave the showroom in your brand new car, there are already 15 tons of carbon dioxide behind you. If you drive a used car, you don't cause another 15,000kg of CO_2 to be emitted. However, as I said, this approach is not for everyone. Many people are simply too busy to take a good care of an old car; and good care is essential because driving an old banger that puffs blue smoke out of its tailpipe is not very green, is it? The car should be in excellent mechanical condition for this method to work.

Air cars

Although in development for more than 20 years, air cars are still more-or-less science fiction. The concept of air cars is being commercialized by a French inventor Guy Negre and his Luxembourg-based company MDI. The first time they announced the possible production of these alternative automobiles was back in 2000. Recently they've partnered up with the Indian car giant Tata to conquer the Asian market. Compressed air is carried on-board in a safe high-pressure tank. The compressed air flows into a chamber where it expands and

If Guy Negre has it his way, AirPod will be the future of our motoring.
(Courtesy MDI Enterprises SA)

simultaneously cools (thermodynamics). Due to expansion the air drives down a piston. The air is reheated by the ambient heat (from the sun) and is forced into the second chamber where the it expands again, driving up a cylinder.

An electric motor is needed to start the car, and to compress the air for the reservoir. An air engine is more efficient because it uses solar energy to heat and expand the air. For the engine to work, though, it needs ambient heat from the sun, even in the winter.

As it is not grid-free, the air car is not 100 per cent environmentally friendly.

Fuel cells

Despite the efforts of President Bush to put America in the forefront of fuel cell developments, nothing really tangible has come out of it. A fuel cell is a sophisticated type of electrochemical battery that converts hydrogen and oxygen into water, and in the process it produces electricity and some heat. It sounds marvellous because we have plenty of oxygen and hydrogen around and having water as a by-product is probably as good as it gets. Still, it's not all perfect. There's no free hydrogen in existence – it must be prepared, compressed and stored. Compressing hydrogen is expensive and consumes energy (generated from fossil fuels). Luckily, there are other types of fuel cells. The one that makes most sense is ethanol (spirit). An ethanol cell requires a platinum-based catalyst, which is very expensive. An alternative nano-surface material is available but, again, it's not cheap. Ethanol cells are work in progress but, once accomplished, they have a huge potential of replacing the carbon-intensive Li-ion batteries in electric cars. Besides, an ethanol-based fuel cell is potentially more efficient than an ethanol combustion engine.

System overview

2 Inverter   5 Compact lithium-ion battery

· Battery used as an auxiliary power source when accelerating

3 Nissan-developed fuel cell stack

1 Motor   4 70MPa high-pressure hydrogen storage cylinder

· Energy generated during deceleration, stored in battery

Layout

That's how Nissan's fuel cell car would look. (Courtesy Nissan)

OMV WASSERSTOFF

Mercedes F-Cell experimental model proudly poses against the background of one of the many hydrogen stations in Germany. (Courtesy DaimlerChrysler)

Biofuels

The two most widespread types of biofuel are bioethanol and biodiesel. They are both derived from sustainable resources like crops, plant material, vegetable oils, organic waste, etc. A biofuel can be used in any internal combustion engine with just minimal modification and tuning work. Although the majority of methods of producing biofuels involve consuming fossil fuels (and burning biofuels in engines still emit CO_2), the idea is that all emissions are offset by the fact that crops 'breathe' large quantities of CO_2 while they grow, thus making the consumption of the biofuel CO_2-negative. More and more people are switching to biofuels in the USA and in several South American countries. In Europe biofuel still struggles to take off mainly due to the lack of free land for growing crops, and thanks to the bureaucrats in the European Union. And, did you know that you can produce diesel from the recycled vegetable oil used at your local fish and chip shop?

four

Electric cars & safety

In the quest to increase the range of electric vehicles, the majority of producers make the vehicles as light as possible and therefore as fragile as possible. Whatever they say and whatever the crash tests show, a smaller car is much less safe than a bigger car. Compromising on safety is not a great idea. It would actually be pretty easy to legalize a cardboard car in Europe by registering it as a quad-bike! The story is different in the USA – the majority of small cars currently produced in China or India (and some that are being developed in Europe) couldn't be made highway-legal and imported into the States. Some of them can get a NEV certification that limits the speed to 25mph (some states are looking to increase it to 35mph) and allows you to use the vehicle on minor public roads (not high-speed public roads or highways).

I'm glad Americans have retained their sanity. They would never put environmental issues above peoples' lives ... or would they? Unfortunately, the egg-shell car makers have found a way around the strict US rules. That's what you do if you want to bend the system and sell a less safe product. Knock one wheel off and register it as a trike. A three-wheeled vehicle is classified as a motorcycle and the rules for automobile certification don't apply. Many buyers are happy that it is possible to trick the system and get a really cheap vehicle, but that doesn't change the fact that they're driving a potentially unsafe vehicle. In the case of a high-speed crash, it will most likely disintegrate.

There will be no more messing about in Canada, though. This next bit is bittersweet, actually. There were two established NEV makers in Canada: ZENN and Dynasty IT. Initially, in 2000 the Canadian government allowed NEVs to be registered and driven. That's when the two companies started making their small cars to order, and between them produced several hundred NEVs. Recently, though, Transport Canada decided to clamp down on the so-called Low Speed Vehicle class, regarding it as a potential threat to road safety. As a result, ZENN switched from making and selling vehicles to supplying electric drivetrains to other manufacturers, and Dynasty IT sold its equipment and know-how to Pakistan. I really feel for Danny Epp, a talented Marine engineer, who created the Dynasty IT car from scratch, but I also understand where Transport Canada is coming from – officials don't feel good about some vehicles being on the road without having passed crash tests. Conventional car manufacturers don't like it either, because the big companies are spending millions to make production cars as safe as possible. If we set too many precedents of letting less safe cars to be driven in the general traffic stream, we'll send out the wrong message to the car manufacturers

Peugeot's take on an NEV, dated 1942. Don't expect a little car like this to save your life in a high-speed accident.
(Courtesy David Saunders via Creative Commons Licence)

and they will decide that we are ready to accept compromises concerning safety. But we are not, are we? Although the number of traffic accidents is gradually creeping up, the fatality rate falls every year – mostly thanks to the technology that now allows car manufacturers to build relatively safe cars in an efficient manner.

The biggest problem with NEVs, trikes and quad bikes is that they co-exist on the public roads with conventional heavy cars. If there were only small and light vehicles in existence, it wouldn't be an issue. Having so many differently-sized and differently-equipped vehicles on the roads simultaneously would be potentially dangerous; and it would be the passengers in smaller cars that would suffer.

If you think I might be biased towards large cars, let's look at two car safety studies, one of which is completely independent.

The first study is by National Highway Traffic Safety Administration (part of the US Department of Transport). In 2003 it finalized a ten-year long study that looked into relations between vehicle weight and fatality risk. This is the verdict of the study: "When two vehicles collide, the laws of physics favour the occupants of the heavier vehicle through momentum conservation. Furthermore, heavy vehicles were in most cases longer, wider and less fragile than light vehicles. In part because of this, they usually had greater crashworthiness, structural integrity and directional stability. They were less rollover-prone and easier for the average driver to control in a panic situation. In other words, heavier vehicles tended to be more crashworthy and less crash-prone."

If we look at fatal crash ratios as compared with total vehicle miles, an interesting picture emerges. Vehicle miles is the total mileage done by all US drivers. Vehicle miles is used in America to convey different statistical reports. By the way, cars in the USA cover roughly 250 billion vehicle miles every month, which is a 100-billion increase over 25 years. Back in 1984, the monthly vehicle miles stood at around 150 billion. The safety reports show that there are 11.56 driver fatalities per billion vehicle miles involving very small cars. But only 3.30 fatalities per billion vehicle miles involving large saloons. According to the US Department of Transport, the safest type of vehicle is a minivan – only 2.76 driver fatalities per billion vehicle miles. It is very difficult to be biased or unbiased about these facts. The data is taken from the official road accident reports.

If you want an independent opinion, there's a study that was carried out by the Highway Loss Data Institute. This is a branch of the US Insurance Institute for Highway Safety and collects data from the nation's insurance brokers. A study is available for 2006-2008 year models. One might think that insurers are afraid of 'speed demons' with large, powerful cars. Of course, you'll be quoted an unfair extra premium if you insure your Ferrari in the USA, but mid- to large-size family cars perform surprisingly well, and incur less than average losses for insurers. The problem starts with the mini and small sectors. There are small cars that are notorious losers of insurance money. On average, the mini and small sector is much more likely to have claims more often, and the claims involve more money or even write-off. But it is not the metal we are worried about, it's the flesh. Claims relating to personal injury protection and medical bills occur more often in relation to mini and small cars. I won't be naming any specific models,

but the aforementioned studies are publicly available. Unfortunately, there are very few European models covered in this particular research.

However, it shouldn't be assumed that all small cars are totally unsafe and dangerous. Those that have performed well in crash tests (Th!nk, Smart, Toyota iQ, and several others) are relatively safe to drive. The Euro NCAP crash test results are displayed as a star rating from one to five. Cars with four or five stars should be relatively safe to drive, although in the Highway Loss Data Institute study there is a four star NCAP car that, regardless of its crash test pass, is infamous with insurers for the health risks it poses to occupants in an event of an accident.

But let's not blame governments or car manufacturers. If there's demand, there will be supply, and there's simply nothing we can do about it (other than banning unsafe cars, one might hope). The life of you and your family is largely in your own hands – it is the choice you make, the risk you are prepared to take.

That's where cars like the Nissan Leaf, Th!nk and Tesla come in handy, showing that it's possible to build an electric car of quite a substantial size without putting the lives of passengers at risk. It is funny, but the size of an electric car has nothing to do with the range. The bigger the car, the more batteries you can fit under the floor – that's why the range of different electric cars is pretty much the same regardless of weight or size. Of course, a larger EV requires a bigger motor but not a great deal bigger. Electric motors generally have a high torque. Driving a very small electric car can save you a little money, but it's never worth it. If you buy an electric car, don't look to downsize. Choose a vehicle that will feel comfortable to you and your family.

five

Topping up – charging your electric car

The lack of charging facilities is often mentioned as the biggest obstacle in switching to electric cars.

After you've done some 100 miles or so, you'll notice that the battery charge level indicator has closed in on the zero mark, reminding you that the car is running out of 'juice.' As it currently stands you can't just pop into a petrol station and 'fill your tank.' Your best bet is to develop the habit of planning your journey ahead. In 99 per cent of cases the only readily available charging point will be your home outlet. Almost any electric car can be plugged into any outlet in the world as long as the voltage and frequency match. If, for instance, you live in the USA and you've happened to have bought a European electric car, you'll need a voltage converter to use it.

Although in theory almost any electric car should be able to do at least 100 miles on one charge, you'll soon find out that the actual mileage will vary according to different factors, such as quality of tarmac, your driving habits, average speed, temperature, etc. Unless you're doing only short runs, you can never be 100 per cent sure you're going to make it back home on your own power (recovery trailers don't count, but I bet they'll appreciate the new business). Currently, long distance, proper intercity travel in pure electric cars is pretty much impossible, as are family motoring vacations. All that would change, however, if, by 2015 a significant proportion of the public embrace the concept of electric cars.

Many countries plan to create large numbers of recharging points. London mayor Boris Johnson wants 7500 charging points by 2013 (a huge increase on the 200-or-so public charging points available in London at the time of writing). In Spain there's a huge incentive, backed by the government, Siemens, and several other private investors, to build a large number of charging stations.

Germany, France and some places in Scandinavia already have a comparably large-scale infrastructure to support electric cars. In the USA charging infrastructure is still in an embryonic stage; even in California – the forefront of all green motoring developments. It looks like San Francisco might become the first American city to introduce a sizeable network of electric car charging facilities. The state Governor Arnold Schwarzenegger wants to create an intercity network of charging stations and battery exchange stations that would enable people to travel 500 miles from Sacramento to San Diego without too much headache. It's just that instead of the usual nine hours and one fuelling stop necessary to get to San Diego driving a petrol car, you'd have to make at least four charging stops and spend extra two hours in an electric car. But is that such a big problem? Walking the same distance would take 12 days ... and that's if you're a fast walker.

Another reason why building public charging points is a challenge is crime/vandalism. The thought of having thousands of easily available outlets begging to be abused is rather worrying. If you can access the plug, so can anyone else regardless of their intention. On-street electricity is a tempting boost for criminals enabling them to use devices that they couldn't possibly use before.

Japanese and Korean colleagues have come up with some truly remarkable alternative methods of charging electric cars. Nissan, in collaboration with a Ukrainian scientific research company, APowerCap, has created a contactless charging system. It's no bigger than a frying pan, and can be integrated under the surface of

Many future parking spaces will have high-voltage charging points installed.
(Courtesy Nissan Motors)

a parking lot. The car needs a receiver under the floor to be able to accept the charge. The system uses the principle of magnetic induction to transmit the charge from the device to the car. A contactless system provides more safety and less oportunity for abuse. The downside of this system (a big one, actually) is that the contactless charging system is only 80 per cent effective. This means that 20 per cent of transmitted energy will disappear in the form of stray magnetic waves.

Nissan is also planning to introduce fast-charge lanes on the major highways, allowing people to charge their electric cars without having to stop. Now, that wouldn't go down well with the people, especially in England where the roads aren't very wide. Can we fit another lane along our highways?

Contactless charger from Nissan – Japanese technology with a touch of Ukrainian know-how.
(Courtesy Nissan Motors)

Well, not without having angry people waving placards by the roadside.

In Korea, the Korean Advanced Institute of Science and Technology, aka KAIST, has devised the On-Line Electric Vehicle (OLEV) system, a rather unusual way to power electric cars around the city. A continuous metal strip is worked into the surface of the road, and the car takes energy in real time as it follows the route. It uses a similar principle to the Nissan system (a magnetic field). To ensure that the line doesn't leak energy when there are no cars following it, a vehicle can have a sensor under the front part of the floor that tells the line "I'm here, give me the juice," and a receiver plate under the rear part of the floor. The digital nature of this system also provides an unexpectedly useful tool in dealing with road-hogs. If, for instance, each On-Line car had a digital signature, the system could be programmed and instructed not to transmit energy to the offending car.

The electricity will be transmitted by magnetic induction. The strips will be comparatively safe for pedestrians to walk over; but dogs, I bet, won't be too appreciative. They never like

hanging around things that emit magnetic fields, and quite rightly so. Animals are much more sensitive to matters which people tend to overlook. Electro-magnetic pollution is an issue in almost every large city. Mobile phone antennae, radio waves, microwave ovens, wi-fi hotspots, and many others are contributing to electro-magnetic chaos. Have you ever wondered why you're getting such frequent headaches during an active day in the city? Electro-magnetic pollution might be a factor. If the On-Line electric vehicle plans go ahead, the level of electro-magnetic pollution will significantly rise.

Currently, the system is not perfect from the point of view of efficiency either. If we're talking about an ideal world, where there are no bumps on the roads and a car can almost touch the surface (1cm clearance), the efficiency of the magnetic transmission reaches 80 per cent; in the real world (12cm clearance), only 60 per cent gets transmitted.

That is a problem, and it will contribute to running costs. We would still have to pay for 100 per cent of electricity but get to use only 60 per

KAIST's On-Line Electric Vehicle undergoing real-life testing. (Courtesy KAIST)

cent. Thus, efficiency of an electric car would fall even further and reach a level where it is much more efficient to walk or roller-skate.

Besides, some will argue that this sort of system robs motoring of its raison d'être – autonomy and mobility.

Then there would be a huge cost to install the metal strips and the infrastructure that goes with them. However, if and when these were installed, they would solve the worst problem we have with electric cars – the limited range. Professors at KAIST have estimated that if 50 per cent of all Korean cars (6 million vehicles) were On-Line, the country would save $3 billion annually on crude oil import. Like the rest of us, Koreans don't want to be economically dependent on the silly 'USA vs Middle East' oil price games.

At the moment it is hard to estimate the price of installing cables in large cities, but this sounds like a potentially good long-term solution. Considering the relatively cheap workforce of South Korea, the sophisticated On-Line system might be paying for itself within

its second year of operation. It is also believed that the two advanced nuclear power stations of South Korea could deal with the surge in demand that would be generated by putting six million electric cars on the streets.

The good thing about this system is that the car doesn't need a huge battery pack. It can now make do with a small pack of only 10kWh or so to go where the lines don't. That's ten times less, cheaper and lighter than with a battery pack of Tesla Roadster. It would mean rebuilding all the major roads in Korea to support so-called On-Line Electric Vehicles. It looks like Koreans have really warmed to this strange and expensive idea, as experiments and tests are going on in various parts of the country.

In the current situation, politicians and city mayors forget about one very important thing. The electric car expansion programme should provide solutions for increasing the reach of electric cars by nurturing convenient inter-city travel. Those living in big cities will have a chance to use one of the thousands of charging points (Mayor Johnson believes that all Londoners will live within a mile of a charging point by 2015) or charge overnight if the car is being parked on a driveway or in a garage. I'm not saying that the charging points shouldn't be built, but there must be another solution for commuters and travellers. The real challenge is to support intercity travel by installing charging outlets in remote petrol stations and parking lots. To involve the private sector in the electric car rush would need the government subsidizing the outlets for the first couple of years of operation. I don't see how we could persuade the owner of a petrol station to install an outlet for electric cars without offering some incentive.

And even that wouldn't immediately allow us to go long distances in electric cars because it takes time to recharge batteries. You now spend on average five minutes in a petrol station, filling up, grabbing a sandwich, etc. With an electric car you'd need to stay there for at least 45 minutes, just whiling away the time. It is by no means a tragedy or the end of the world if you're just travelling. However, being delayed by almost an hour during a business trip is something that many of us wouldn't be too happy about.

The current technology of batteries does require several hours (6 to eight in many cases) to reach full charge level. On the other hand even the less advanced batteries can get a significant amount of charge in 45 minutes to one hour, allowing the car to travel for another couple of dozen miles.

Fast-charge systems are something that many companies are working on as a matter of priority. Theoretically, there are systems that can fast-charge a battery to 80 per cent charge level within 15 minutes or less. However, that sort of advanced technology is not widely available today or tomorrow. Either it resembles sci-fi too much, is too expensive, or requires mega voltage to make it happen.

In order to accept fast-charge, the whole electric grid should be revamped. It will collapse if we all start fast-charging our electric cars. Your home outlet will have a maximum power of 3kW or even less if you're on a 110-volt supply. 3kW is nowhere near to what is necessary in order to fast-charge a battery. So, in order to fully recharge the oversized battery of Tesla Roadster (53kWh capacity) you'd need to wait for 17 hours. A battery of an average electric car (25kWh capacity) would take roughly eight hours to charge from a 3kW outlet.

To think that somebody would come and upgrade our electric grid ... well, no-one would come. It would cost at least $1200 to upgrade the conventional home wiring system for a safe use of a domestic fast-charger. There are two ways around this. One is waiting for the battery technology to improve, and the other one is to install high-voltage charging points. Putting a peak power of half a Megawatt through the batteries would be crazy, the batteries could overheat, and even blow up!

Battery technology is improving. Nano-augmented surfaces permit accepting the charge a few times faster than conventional batteries. The downside of nanotechnology is that it is still relatively expensive. Although you might hear the news that this or that company has developed a battery that can enable the car to cover 300 or 500 miles between charges, the technology is still too risky and expensive for anyone to attempt transferring it from science fiction to the real world of production. That's why you'd struggle to find an electric car confident about covering more than 100 miles on a single charge.

American company AltairNano from Nevada has apparently created an advanced Li-ion battery that is more powerful than a conventional Li-ion, and will charge quicker. Instead of graphite electrodes, AltairNano is using nano-augmented lithium-titanate oxide-based anode material.

Company SSC Green Inc claims it can demonstrate how to charge an electric car in ten minutes. Even if we assume that the technology to put tens of kilowatt hours into a battery within minutes exists, the infrastructure to support the quick-charge does not. High voltage is needed to quick-charge anything. Your UK 230-volt outlet just won't cut it. Yes, OK, high-voltage outlets can be installed in service centres and fuel stations, but it will be difficult to safeguard the electric car owners from electrocution and arc flash (a severe electric blast that occurs between high voltage and low voltage sources due to the resistance of air).

Regardless of what the start-up battery guru companies tell you, the electric cars that you buy today and within the next couple of years will still need six to ten hours to be fully charged. Anything beyond that in the current situation is unsafe, and none of the large car manufacturers would put potentially hazardous technology inside their mass-market cars.

One possible way out of this is slot-in batteries. Imagine; you drive into a petrol station and somebody replaces your car's depleted batteries with a new, fully-charged set. In that case the electric car manufacturers would need to agree on adopting a unified worldwide standard for batteries, which they would never do because everyone thinks their batteries are the best. Nevertheless, it is expected that several of the models that are about to be made available for the public will have easy access to the battery pack (through the side or from below the floor). If the slot-in system ever gets rolled out, it is unclear who would own the batteries, and how it would be made possible to have a fair deal for everyone. Batteries become less efficient with age, and it is highly probable that your car would get a replacement of a sordid old set of batteries next time you went for a slot-in option.

six

Electric car conversions

Ever since the dawn of the motoring era, man has tried to improve his cars by adding (or in some cases removing) components and features. We never seem to be quite content with mass-produced cars. The design is not exciting enough, there's not enough power, speed, bling, etc. There are people who convert their 'boring' petrol cars into pedal cars, solar cars, biofuel cars, natural gas cars, heap of rusty metal cars, and so on. Now, with the general public inclined more towards the green stuff, electric car conversion is the new fashion.

Although the practice of converting a conventional petrol car into an electric car is not as difficult as it might sound, it is more common to find it done in the USA (Europeans are, perhaps, less keen on getting their hands dirty). Two factors explain the US domination in this area: relatively few Europeans have their own garage or the space to rebuild a car; and the necessary components cost

more there than they do in America. If the petrol car is of decent quality and low mileage, it's possible to recoup some of the investment by selling the unwanted parts. The engine in its entirety has to go, and you might get a few hundred pounds for a good engine on the second-hand market.

The exhaust system, fuel pump, and fuel tank are removed, though the transmission usually stays. As we discovered earlier, an electric car can do without a gearbox because it produces almost constant power and torque, regardless of revs. Still, it's a good idea to leave the transmission in place and make it work as a reduction gear to make the car go more smoothly, and to be able to control the speed better. In an electric car conversion, the original transmission is usually fixed down to be constantly in first, second or third gear, depending on the weight of the car and some other factors. With a manual transmission, it's relatively easy to lock all the gears but second and reverse, meaning that you'd have a gearbox with three modes: drive, neutral, and reverse.

In some cases the only way to get reverse is to have the motor's polarity switched, and going in reverse electronically. An AC motor can do it without a problem. With a DC motor (and the majority of home electric car conversions use a DC system because it's cheaper and simpler) it's not so straightforward. A DC motor can go in reverse, but by doing so it will make the brushes wear out more quickly. Therefore, many experts suggest that DC conversions use a simple mechanical transmission to handle the reverse manually.

Looks like a normal MG car. It is a normal car and it drives like a normal car ... only a little greener. (Courtesy PI Marketing Limited (UK))

With an AC motor reverse is much easier. It only needs a reduction gear. The reverse switch will be electronic.

OK, back to our conversion. So, the car has lost its motor and some other parts. The main two parts going under the hood are the electric motor and controller. The controller is an essential thing – it is a mediator between the battery pack and the motor. It will control how much power the motor

gets. Additional small electric motors are now necessary if you want your power steering and air conditioner back (this is optional and, trust me, not really necessary) and more motors for the water pump and brakes. A simple water heater will be necessary to heat the interior – unless you want to pinch Audi's idea and install a miniature heat pump.

The biggest challenge of every electric car converter is where to put the batteries. The majority of conversions will have the simplest and cheapest lead batteries. They are heavier than Li-ion batteries and provide less range but it is rarely recommended for a newbie to start tinkering with Li-ion batteries. When converting a petrol car you must be ready for a compromise. Much of the luggage space will have to be abandoned for batteries. It is possible to arrange the batteries under the floor of a car, but in many cases this is not advisable because it can affect the structural soundness and safety.

Financially, it's much cheaper to convert a petrol car into an electric car (if you already own a petrol car) than to buy a brand new electric car. In the UK you won't qualify for the government's 2011 incentive, though, because that's meant to give the new industry a boost and get people to buy the cars. It's aimed more at the maker and less at the consumer. However, an electric car conversion will qualify for zero road tax from now on, saving you some £200 every year.

In the USA, people looking to have a foothold on the green motoring thing can apply for an IRS tax refund. But one must hurry, however, because later in 2011 the tax credit policy will be reviewed, and it's possible that conversions registered after December 31, 2011 won't qualify for a tax break, or the tax break will be reduced. Currently, you're entitled to ten per cent of the money you spend on the conversion. Thus, if you buy a $10,000-worth conversion kit, you are entitled to $1000 money back. If you can also prove that you've spent money on resources and man-hours, in some cases you can claim it as costs and increase your tax break. Check with an accountant or tax advisor, though, because the rules are different from state-to-state. High-spec conversions are covered up to $4000 money back. So, you can opt for a sports car conversion, spend $40,000 and still get a tax refund. There won't be many $40,000-jobs in the electric car conversion department, though, because the majority of people going for a conversion are doing this simply to be able to wave a finger at the petrol station workers as they drive past on their electric traction.

Another benefit of converting to electricity is escaping the battery fee. As I already mentioned, in most cases you don't get to own the batteries if you buy a brand new electric vehicle. The batteries are leased and a monthly fee is usually involved. With a conversion, once you've bought the batteries from the marine shop or wherever, you own them, and the next time you splash out on batteries is when they become wrecked.

Those really considering tackling car conversion from scratch should probably buy a book dedicated to electric car conversions. All the kits are accompanied by a user manual. Converting a car is not rocket science, and most of the people will find this experience interesting and refreshing. The average timescale for a kitted conversion, if you work on weekends and put in some weekday evening hours as well, is two months. Doing a conversion from scratch might take a

little longer because you need time to plan everything and source the parts.

Fixing the electric motor to the original transmission is another big challenge. You will need an adaptor plate that is different for every model. Marque-specific conversion kits are available only for the most popular mass-produced cars. If you are skipping the kits altogether or converting a model that doesn't have a kit available, somebody will have to make the adaptor plate for you. It has to be strong enough to hold the motor in place and fix it to the transmission properly. If making the plate on your own, factor in the vibration and moment of force. The motor will do the best to jump out of the car and your task is to prevent it from doing so.

Another important thing is to make the electrical system safe. A set of fuses and a proper master switch, that can mechanically disconnect the batteries should something go wrong, will do the job.

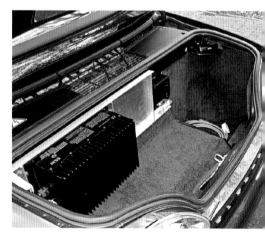

A converted MG – despite fitting the charging system in the boot, there's still some space left for luggage. That yellow under the grille is a battery pack.
(Courtesy PI Marketing Limited (UK))

The fuel dial is then replaced with a simple voltmeter so that you know when it's necessary to recharge the batteries.

Once the first stage of conversion is finished, there is always room for improvement ... that's if there's any room left after installing the batteries. The usual extra thing that is added to the electric car conversion is a regenerative braking system. Once flexible solar panels become readily available, it will be possible to mount them on top of the roof, and potentially cut the electricity bill by up to 20 per cent.

A full electric car kit including the batteries will cost you between £5000 to £8000 depending on specs and the model you're converting. If you're getting someone else to work for you, count in the man-hours as well, and that's where it probably ceases to be an economically sound procedure. For those who have significant experience in DIY and who can source the parts on their own without using the kit-car companies, the conversion process will be cheaper.

There are certain running costs involved in driving a converted electric car. Firstly, there's the cost of electricity you consume to charge the batteries. Secondly, you have to factor in battery wear. Lead-based units will last a maximum of four years or 30,000 miles. Li-ion batteries might go twice as long. A new set of lead batteries for a family-size car will cost you at least £1500. Therefore, each mile you drive will cost you another £0.05 on top of the electricity bill. It is still cheaper than driving a petrol car.

Neil Hutchinson from PI Marketing (you can see photos of his MG conversion in this chapter) is happy with his new electric car conversion. He estimates that the conversion will have paid for itself within 5 years.

What is good about electric car conversions is that you don't have to change your driving habits and downsize to a less comfortable car. You can stick with your own car and just make it more viable both economically and environmentally. Like driving a large car but cannot afford to provide for its greedy V8? Choose a bigger electric motor and at the cost of a shorter range (compared to a smaller and lighter car) save your beloved car from the scrapyard. Besides, it is not set in stone that the range of a large car conversion will be shorter. A larger car can obviously house more batteries. In other words, you don't have to become a victim of the small car propaganda. If you like large cars, don't feel guilty about it. Just bear in mind that car conversion will work only for city commuters because, whichever car you convert, its range will still be lower than that of a factory-made electric car because you simply don't have all the sophisticated tech and know-how at your fingertips.

The idea of converting a mass-produced car into something else is not new. We are never surprised by hearing about an LPG (liquid propane gas) conversion. Going electric is as normal as going LPG; it is only less common because it's more difficult to switch to electricity, and the whole electric car idea is barely taking off right now. But trust me, there will be an electric car conversion boom in Europe within the next couple of years. The first signs of this boom are showing in America with conversion companies appearing everywhere.

seven

Electric car catalogue

In this section, we'll take a look at the most exciting production cars and pre-production prototypes – cars that are almost ready and cars that are being tested and tweaked. There are some really interesting models in this section, and, although you should take the majority of promises with a pinch of salt, there are cars to be watched. Many production dates will be missed, estimated retail prices pushed up, and travelling ranges cut 'due to technological limitations,' but, we shouldn't judge them too harshly. After all, the electric car is a brand new industry, and it will take time to mould this idea into something that the public would unanimously appreciate.

Alleweder Velomobile
Let's start this chapter with some light refreshment. Alleweder is a velomobile; it is the little known competitor of the much-touted Twike.

Built by Lohmeyer Light Vehicles in Germany, it is quite popular locally but a mystery beyond the borders. Including the light convertible roof with windshield (you guessed right, the roof is not included in the standard equipment) and the battery pack, the price for an Alleweder is between 6000 to 10,000 Euros, depending on equipment and battery size. It is also available as a DIY kit, making the purchase even cheaper. Much cheaper than a Twike, but then Alleweder is a single-seater and it offers even less protection from the atmosphere and other traffic. It is really quite fragile, but compared to a bicycle (I'd never promote riding bikes in busy city traffic but there will be people opting for this anyway) the Alleweder is more prominent and at least has some sort of a shell to encase the rider.

The Alleweder is an amazingly simple and light vehicle. Including batteries, it weighs around 60kg thanks to its all-fibreglass body (this fibreglass

Alleweder is an expensive velomobile with a small electric wheel-hub motor. (Courtesy Alleweder.eu)

body is one of the reasons why the Alleweder is not cheap).

When it comes to saving money on your road bill or reducing your carbon footprint, the Alleweder is a little marvel. It consumes ten times less energy than an electric car. Hence, even with a small battery it has a range of 100 miles, and, unlike an electric car, it won't die on you once the battery goes flat. You can pedal it home using your own power. To achieve the top speed of 30mph the motor on its own won't be enough, you will have to pedal too.

It is powered by a hub motor installed directly onto the wheel. A motor like this weighs only 6kg. Light vehicles may not worry about the unsprung mass, the fact that the wheel is heavy won't affect its handling too much.

Vehicles like the Alleweder and Twike are obviously not for everyone. There is only a certain amount of people who might enjoy and fully appreciate an electric velomobile. From those who

could (students and green activists for instance), the majority cannot afford to spend thousands of Euros; they're even struggling to save for a bicycle.

Technical specifications

Motor power	0.5kW
Motor torque	n/a
Battery capacity	2kWh
Estimated range	100 miles
Max speed	30mph

Aptera

Despite the continuous rumours that Aptera Motors is dying, it seems to be pretty much alive. If the US Federal government's refusal to give the company a low-interest loan, based on the fact that the Aptera was a three-wheel vehicle, didn't kill it, probably nothing will.

The Aptera project started out in 2006 as a computer-rendered image of a car with an extremely low drag coefficient. The demonstration model that followed didn't deliver on the drag

Although it looks like it wants to fly, the Aptera is wingless. (Courtesy Jason H Harper, jasonhharper.com)

coefficient initially promised, but still, the production model Aptera 2e, with its 0.15 drag coefficient, is probably the world's most aerodynamically advanced passenger car. It's body is even more streamlined than the Solectria Sunrise.

However, there is a trade-off – the car doesn't look much like a car. It's more of a Cessna that's driving around looking for its lost wings. Although it looks like an aircraft, wings were never part of the deal, hence the name Aptera – it means 'wingless' in Greek.

The Aptera is touted as the most efficient passenger car in the world, consuming only 0.08kWh per mile (the majority of electric cars will consume around 0.25kWh per mile) which amounts to only a couple of cents per mile.

2009 was a difficult year for Aptera Motors. After the US Federal government refused to give it a $184 million low-interest loan, the company launched a convoluted lobby campaign to get the three-wheel cars included in the loan scheme. Now it has reapplied, and there is no reason why it shouldn't get the money this time around. If the loan is granted, the production of the Aptera 2e is a certainty. According to the company's CEO, Paul Wilbur, it's

a certainty anyway – the easy or the hard way, he would get there eventually. The company is known to have lured a couple of high-flying investors on-board, as well as started building an original equipment and outsourcing chain in the USA. Currently, the plan is to start producing the Apteras later in 2011.

Although the retail price hasn't been revealed (and it might be as low as $25,000), the company is taking $500 deposits from residents of California (yes, currently the pre-ordering campaign is limited to Californians). If 2011 sees a successful production launch, the Aptera could arrive in Europe in 2012.

The Aptera sounds like a safe car: the two-seater interior is enclosed in a safety capsule, and there are crunch zones at the front and rear to absorb collision energy. Aptera Motors says that the car's fiberglass body can withstand the weight of two elephants on the roof. The impressive cargo compartment can hold up to 15 shopping bags.

Public acceptance of the Aptera 2e might be an issue. Although it's a great and efficient vehicle, some could find its looks unacceptable. One should understand, though, that the way the car looks isn't dictated by the fancy of the designer – it is the unusual aerodynamic body (and the ultra-low 800kg weight) that makes the Aptera as efficient as it is. My biggest concern with the Aptera is its rear wheel. I don't know about the USA, but in Britain its casing would probably fail at the very first speed bump, and I'm not even mentioning the potholes!

Technical specifications

Motor power	82kW
Motor torque	314Nm
Battery capacity	n/a
Estimated range	100 miles
Max speed	80mph

Pre-assembled in Oxford, finished in Munich, shipped back to England for tests – BMW Mini E.
(Courtesy BMW)

BMW Mini E

I remember criticising this car for its awkward method of assembly. The Minis are assembled in Oxford, and then shipped to Munich, where they are fitted with the electric drivetrain and other bits. With a factory so well equipped and staffed with top professionals, it seems odd that the cars have to make the 1580-mile return journey to receive parts that could just as well be fitted in Oxford. It is uneconomical, and adds to grey energy, which is already very high for the cars. I expect that once the Mini E goes on a mass-scale production, something will be done about this. Otherwise your 'green' car would need to do a 1000-mile run on 100 per cent-renewable energy just to justify its Oxford-Munich journey.

Early in 2009 BMW leased out several hundreds of Minis to selected customers for field tests. The level of interest was tremendous. The company managed a 10,000-long waiting list of people ready to pay 600 Euros per month for a chance to drive a Mini E.

So far BMW is happy with the field tests, and sooner or later the car will hit the production lines.

There is a nasty surprise concerning the Mini, though; it's a two-seater. The back of the car is occupied by batteries. BMW's press release states that: "The car will initially be available as a two-seater"; apparently, this means that BMW is looking into the possibility of reclaiming the rear seats for human use by downsizing the batteries, or shifting them under the floor. As a two-seater it's really not worth much. The idea behind the Mini, right from 1959, was to provide four seats within a limited space.

Mini E is a front-wheel drive car and has an AC motor producing 150kW power. Why does a small car have such a big motor if its maximum speed is electronically limited to 95mph and the 0-60mph acceleration electronically delayed to 10.5 seconds in order to prevent burnout? I hope BMW knows what it's doing, and I don't really consider the Mini E an accomplished car. After all, it's still in the test phase, and once the test results come back home I expect the car will undergo a major revision, and possibly gain the two missing seats.

Meanwhile, in Lone Mountain, Nevada, an alternative electric Mini, under the moniker of LIV Flash, is being made to order. Although it has a shorter range than the factory model, it is a proper four-seater. Made by a company called Li-ion Motors Corp (formerly known as Hybrid Technologies Nevada), it is an original Oxford chassis fitted with the American know-how. The company has a nice array of professional electric car conversions on offer. Chrysler PT Cruiser (LIV Surge), Smart Car (LIV Dash), Toyota Auris (LIV Wise), electric chopper-style motorbike, and amazing three original models developed in-house. It will be interesting to see how the factory-born Mini E competes with its little American cousin LIV Flash.

Technical specifications (factory model)

Motor power	150kW
Motor torque	220Nm
Battery capacity	35kWh
Estimated range	155 miles
Max speed	95mph

Technical specifications (Nevada)

Motor power	n/a
Motor torque	n/a
Battery capacity	n/a
Estimated range	100 miles
Max speed	80mph

Bolloré Blue Car

Also known as the Pininfarina B0, this is a collaboration between three companies: Italian design guru Pininfarina; French industrial giant Bolloré; and EDF (Electricite de France). Bolloré is a rich and influential company specializing in security devices. It has made millions producing turnstiles,

Bolloré Blue Car – there is serious investment behind this solar electric car. (Courtesy Bluecar.fr)

alarms, and James Bond-esque personal identification systems.

The Blue Car is rather innovative. As you can see from the technical specifications, it promises a longer range than many other electric cars. Bolloré and EDF set up a dedicated company, BatScap, that would work just on the battery technology. It took 15 years to come up with a new concept: a lithium metal polymer battery which would take up less space than solid lithium batteries due to the ultra thin technology used. Anodes and cathodes are made from an ultra-thin metal foil, and the electrolyte is a solid chunk of lithium salt in a polyoxyethylene mass. The battery pack developed by BatScap is five times lighter than a similar liquid state battery. It's probably the first meant-for-production electric car with supercapacitors on-board. These perform the immediate energy storage to take regenerative braking energy and electricity generated by the photovoltaic panel on the roof. The use of supercapacitors in this case means that the main battery will have fewer short-term loads and no energy surges as the car accelerates. The sudden high-energy consumption for accelerating is one of the things that usually reduces the battery life. The Blue Car has apparently solved that problem.

Although currently the Blue Car is nothing more than one of many cars available for pre-order, it's hard to imagine how Bolloré could not succeed. The BatScap division that deals only with battery technology has more than 150 employees. In the long run, having its own dedicated battery team might play a key part in the future because the insufficient energy storage of batteries is the one biggest problem with electric cars.

Considering all the work and hi-tech applications that have gone into developing the Blue Car, it would be unusual if it was democratically priced. It will probably be rather expensive. Currently, the company is considering leasing out a test batch of the electric cars. A 300 Euro deposit is being taken from people expressing a firm interest in driving a Blue Car in the near future.

Despite its compact size, the Blue Car is a proper four-seater car, and the fact that Pininfarina has worked on it means that it has a design value associated with it.

Technical specifications

Motor power	50kW
Motor torque	n/a
Battery capacity	various
Estimated range	150 miles
Max speed	80mph

Chevrolet Volt

The Volt is one of the most eagerly awaited new cars in the world. So much has been said about the Volt that one is beginning to wonder where the truth ends and the legend begins.

The Volt is built on the experience General Motors had with its EV1 experiment. Some would say that was an unsuccessful experiment, but GM certainly doesn't feel that way.

The Volt is a unique car, in the sense that it's neither an electric car nor

One of the most awaited cars in the world – the Chevrolet Volt. (Courtesy GM)

a hybrid. The Volt is an extended-range vehicle powered by a 120kWh electric motor. Its battery is limited in size. Its main block has just 8kWh capacity providing a range of 40 miles. After the electricity is used up, an on-board internal combustion generator kicks in to make electricity for the motor. As the petrol engine doesn't directly power the wheels, the Volt cannot be classified as a hybrid (you don't call a diesel-electric locomotive a hybrid, do you?). Although you can't classify it as a hybrid, its essence is close to the other plug-in hybrids – to provide a limited range on electricity and have a conventional add-on power that would set people for a longer journey.

Technically, General Motors has moved away from the EV1 concept quite significantly. The volume of batteries has gone down from nine cubic feet to three cubic feet.

Seating capacity has increased from two to four. The Volt is a good-size family hatchback. Moving away from the achievements of the EV1, General Motors has lost some of the aerodynamic quality of the old car. Between a funny shape and normal design, GM has chosen the latter. Looking like a normal car, the Volt's drag coefficient is as per any other car.

The interior of the Volt looks more expensive than it actually is. (Courtesy GM)

Technical specifications

Motor power	120kWh
Motor torque	n/a
Battery capacity	8kWh
Estimated range	40/300 miles
Max speed	100mph

Citroën C1 ev'ie

The ev'ie is a glorified conversion of the standard Citroën C1. The conversion is done by a British company; Electric Car Corporation. The team comprises a bunch of professionals, people connected with the fleet management giant Trafficmaster, an ex-Conservative Party Whip, a former sales guru of Ford Motor Company, and a member of the board of London Taxi International – the infamous company that has transferred some of the last independent UK motoring jobs to China. Having such a pro line-up means that they won't stop at the ev'ie, and an expansion is due to follow soon.

Pricewise, GM wants to position the new hatchback in the mid range of the market to enable mass following and high-volume sales. It's expected that, in the US, the car will cost less than $37,500, so that after deducting the $7500 Federal tax credit, consumers would enjoy the new car for less than $30,000. I believe that, unlike the small electric car start-ups, GM will be able to keep the price promise even though it would have to operate the whole Volt endeavour on a significant loss for the next few years (simply because pushing the smaller carmakers out of the market will pay off in the long-term). Despite the fact that the hybrid sales are temporarily dwindling, GM is confident that the Volt would sell well. Before a really big breakthough in battery technology happens, it seems that plug-in hybrids are the most sensible alternatives to gas-guzzlers.

In Europe, the car will be sold under the name of Opel/Vauxhall Ampera. There is a suggestion that the cars meant for European market (including Opel-branded) would be assembled at Ellesmere Port in England. Now this is unofficial, but if it comes true, it would mean more jobs around Merseyside.

The conversion process has been similar to what I had described earlier, though done to a much higher standard. The original C1's gearbox is left in place, fixed into the third gear. Engineless cars arrive from the Czech Republic, where all the petrol C1s are

Citroën C1 ev'ie – a professional conversion made by the Electric Car Corporation. (Courtesy theelectriccarcorporation.co.uk)

assembled, and the conversion is done in Flitwick, UK, at the ECC's production facility.

The base price is £18,550 making it one of the most affordable electric cars in the UK. As you may know, the base price for a petrol Citroën C1 is £8495, and a diesel will cost £10,650. So you see, there is a difference. However, considering the savings and the 2011 incentive, an ev'ie might be a good purchase. Both three- and five-door electric models are available. The ECC has estimated that cost of fully charging the ev'ie from a standard 13 ampere socket is just 95 pence in the UK. It usually takes no more than six hours to recharge the batteries.

Technical specifications

Motor power	30kW
Motor torque	n/a
Battery capacity	various
Estimated range	75 miles
Max speed	60mph

City El

The City El is yet another strange, single-seater three-wheeler from Europe (this time famous for having no door). Access to the interior is granted through a hinged top section. The vehicles are made in Germany and sold locally, as well as in France and the Netherlands. Unlike the Twike, this is not a velomobile. The base price is EUR10,000 but you will want to spend a few hundred on top for upgrades and features. The manufacturer claims that the City El consumes only about 0.08kWh per mile (three times less than a full-size electric car). This estimate sounds plausible – the three-wheeler weighs only 260kg, including the batteries.

Technical specifications

Motor power	4.5kW
Motor torque	n/a
Battery capacity	various
Estimated range	50-75 miles
Max speed	40mph

Some think the City El is not very safe because of its size. There are also concerns about the awkward entry. (Courtesy smiles-world.de)

Commercial electric vehicles

As soon as you mention electric cars, many people will think about the old milk floats, golf cars, and yellow tow tractors. Fair enough! What I really want to draw your attention to is that electric cars have been around for decades. Just like any other invention, they have made a big technological leap. Commercial electric vehicles continue to attract new businesses. While some businessmen are driven to electrify their fleet by environmental concerns, the majority will switch to electric vehicles to save money.

If you consider a company involved in daily deliveries or running errands and servicing various objects around town, it makes a lot of sense to use electric vehicles. The savings are more than obvious. Although an electric van might be a bit more expensive than a similar petrol vehicle, in the long run it is possible to save lots of money on fuel bills and road tax.

The electric car craze is not only about the road-going cars. There are little known manufacturers that make lovely industrial vehicles: personnel carriers, tow tractors, utility vehicles, for example. Owners of large factories, and people looking after territories (gardens, stately homes) should consider electric vehicles. If the vehicle never leaves the site, the range is not an issue. You cannot possibly cover more than 30 miles a day running errands within a factory yard.

Bradshaw Electric Vehicles is one of the largest and oldest manufacturers of industrial electric vehicles in the UK. It started back in 1960 as a dealership for Taylor Dunn, and built its very own first electric vehicle in 1990. Today its world-renowned tow tractors and burden carriers are used in factories, industrial estates, and airports. It also makes golf carts and small utility vehicles popular with gardeners and cricket grounds.

Taylor Dunn is still going strong, having made 'green' vehicles since 1949. To complement its bespoke range of personnel carriers and other industrial vehicles, it has recently introduced a range of small road-going minitrucks, with a maximum range of 40 miles and maximum load capacity of 1300kg.

Bradshaw tow tractor designed and built in the UK. A boom is expected in the sector of industrial electric vehicles.
(Courtesy Bradshaw Electric Vehicles, bradshawelectricvehicles.co.uk)

A small crew carrier by Taylor Dunn.
(Courtesy Omega Parts, omega-parts.com)

Fisker Karma – a luxury four-door with bags of character. (Courtesy fiskerautomotive.com)

Fisker Karma

Henrik Fisker is a Danish-born American car designer whose name is usually associated with Aston Martin and the initial phases of designing the Tesla Model S. It's still unclear how Fisker and Tesla drifted apart, but soon after they fell out, Tesla took the matter to the court claiming that Henrik Fisker worked on the Model S only in order to gain access to the company's production secrets. Apart from losing money on court expenses, Tesla didn't gain anything. The hearing was ruled in favour of Fisker Automotive.

Currently, it looks like there's not much in common with the Fisker Karma and the Tesla Model S, the former being a sort of a plug-in hybrid while the latter is an all-electric car. The Fisker Karma is really more related to the Chevy Volt than to any other electric car.

The Karma has a 50-mile range from its limited size Li-ion battery pack, but it also has a two-litre internal combustion engine onboard to generate electricity when the batteries are out. It also has a third alternative source of electricity: a photovoltaic element

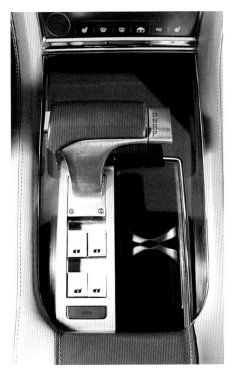

Interior is a fusion of different styles. Only expensive and high-quality materials are used. (Courtesy Fisker Automotive)

If the saloon (sedan) proves popular, a convertible version will soon follow.
(Courtesy Fisker Automotive)

on its roof. Fisker is being realistic about the capabilities of the roof panel. Providing there is enough sunlight, the photovoltaic roof will power the sophisticated climate control unit, as well as some other ancillary on-board systems. Plus, it can provide an extra five-mile range every week. Insignificant on its own, I know, but it all adds up – 260 free miles per year plus savings on operating the climate control, which would otherwise take the energy straight from the batteries. Besides, Fisker Automotive has plans to provide solar panels for the homes and gardens of the prospective car owners so that they could embrace the 'green-home-green-car' philosophy.

The Karma is all about luxury and comfort. Although the car is huge (almost five metres in length), it has only four seats, but these are comfortable and the luggage compartment is bigger than that in competitors' cars. The car is unique in the fact that only the design has been produced by Fisker: everything else is a result of a brilliant outsourcing campaign. Almost everything, from the simple knobs to the high-tech drive technology, has been outsourced to companies in the USA and Europe, thus cutting development costs by a third. So you see, the

start-ups are much more efficient than those of the traditional Detroit-style car manufacturers, who would rather commission a brainstorming team to design a door handle than outsource it to anyone.

Although the Karma is described as a sportscar, it promises to go quietly as well. The driver will be able to select between two modes of driving. The first mode is Stealth Drive, which is the quiet economy mode for optimal relaxed and efficient driving. By flipping the second paddle behind the steering wheel, the car will switch to Sport Drive, which will access the full power of the vehicle. The hybrid drivetrain is developed by another California-based company, Quantum Technologies. QT is also known to be fiddling with hydrogen fuel systems, so I wouldn't be at all surprised if it was contemplating a hydrogen propulsion system.

The car is scheduled to enter production in the second part of 2010 for the American market, and early 2011 for Europe. The summer of 2010 will see a large North American travelling retail exhibition of Fisker Karma visiting 42 locations in the USA, and several places in Canada, to lure potential buyers across the North America. The Karma will be produced in Finland, in the Valmet factory that currently assembles Th!nk electric cars and Porsche gas-guzzlers. Considering the Karma is American technology materialized in Europe, at least the quality should be top notch.

The estimated retail price of the Fisker Karma is $87,000. Currently, pre-orders are being taken and the amount of deposit is $5000 (the deposit for a convertible version is $25,000 – obviously the company is trying to raise money for development – and the pre-order list of the limited edition signature car is already full). The company has received quite a few pre-orders, and the main reason the Karma attracts interest is its unusual appearance.

Technical specifications

Motor power	2x150kW
Motor torque	1300Nm
Battery capacity	22kWh
Estimated range	50/300 miles
Max speed	125mph

Fisker cars will be assembled in the Valmet factory, Finland, alongside the famous Th!nk car. (Courtesy Think EV)

Ford Focus Electric

Unlike other large manufacturers, Ford is prioritising the commercial vehicle sector. Its electric car expansion will begin with introducing the Ford Transit Connect Electric pick-up in 2011. Ford Focus Electric, now extensively featured in the media, will follow in 2012. By 2013, Ford will have extended its eco-range to five electric and hybrid-electric cars. The company announced recently that it's allocating $450 million for its electric car program in 2010. And that's in Michigan alone, where Ford is building a new plant dedicated to producing electric cars and hybrids. And then there's a hefty low-interest loan provided by the Department of Energy in the US, but the biggest part of that will go towards making the petrol engines more environmentally friendly.

Ford isn't exactly a newbie in the field of electric cars. In 1913 Henry Ford, together with the electric guru Thomas Edison, worked on an electric car concept. Although two experimental models were produced, it never came to anything. Henry Ford with his business acumen obviously

Ford Focus Electric – a successful collaboration between Ford and Magna. (Courtesy Ford)

had a hunch that the electric car era was about to end. If the Ford-Edison collaboration had gone on there would have been a Model T Electric, but that never happened.

After the Henney Kilowatt went bust, Ford had a short stint of playing with a small electric car called Comuta. Despite having only four lead-acid batteries under the floor, it had a 40-mile range.

Before starting to develop its own electric cars meant for production, Ford had a brief collaboration with the Norwegian Th!nk.

The Ford Focus is one of those electric cars that is actually an electric car conversion. According to Ford it isn't because the company is too lazy to produce an all-new design. It is merely trying to oppose the current fashion of making the eco-cars flashy. Driving some of the newest electric or hybrid cars you're screaming: "Look, I'm driving a green car." Although there's nothing wrong with driving green, some shyer drivers might get spooked away from the idea. Ford thinks that many people don't want such attention, hence it's giving them a car that looks exactly as its petrol cousin.

This also allows Ford to cut the expenses, making the Focus as affordable as possible. The company is targeting the $20,000-$25,000 bracket in the USA, which will be cheaper than the Nissan Leaf, and significantly cheaper than the Chevy Volt.

The electric technology behind the Ford Focus Electric was developed by Canadian automotive component maker Magna. It had converted a petrol Ford Focus into an electric car using its own unique drivetrain technology. When the car was presented to Ford management, the Americans were pleasantly surprised, and soon decided to enter into a collaboration with Magna.

Although Ford holds a licence to Magna's technology, it is non-exclusive, which means that other companies can use the same drivetrain. Magna really needs this to be a success because it's finished 2009 with a half-billion dollar operational loss.

If Ford really manages to open its production lines in time, the Focus Electric can become a strong contender. The petrol Focus is a solid, proper-size car that is considered quite safe and reliable. And if the company really keeps down the costs, it's likely that a 4.3-metre Focus will be significantly cheaper than some of the independently-produced eggshell cars.

In 2010, several Focus Electric test units will arrive in the UK for extensive field tests run by Scottish Energy and University of Strathclyde. If the tests prove to be successful, Ford might produce up to 10,000 cars annually starting from 2012. Although it seems that it's really committed to the electric car idea, some people from the Ford camp still think that electric cars will be nothing more than a narrow niche market for the next decade or so.

Technical specifications

Motor power	100kW
Motor torque	n/a
Battery capacity	23kWh
Estimated range	100 miles
Max speed	85mph

Ford Transit Connect Electric

Although Ford and Magna seem to be on the same wavelength when it concerns the passenger cars, they won't be collaborating on Ford's breakthrough into the electric car market. The Transit Connect electric pick-up was initially a product of Ford/Smith Electric alliance. Now that Smith has moved on to manufacture its own commercial vehicle, Ford has found

Ford Transit Connect E – its optimal size and performance are bang on for a small business or a delivery company. (Courtesy Ford)

a new partner in Solectria (now Azure Dynamics) – the company behind the unique Solectria Sunrise (see the History chapter). I think Ford and Smith drifting apart is actually beneficial for both companies. Smith wants to concentrate on large vehicles while Ford is playing it safe and probing the market with the entry-level pick-up.

Many small businesses are eagerly awaiting the Connect Electric, but whether their enthusiasm remains depends on the final retail price.

The Transit Connect has recently received a five-star crash test rating from the US National Highway Traffic Safety Administration. Those who have tested the Connect Electric note that the car is not too different from its petrol relative – simple and minimalist.

Technical specifications

Motor power	50kW
Motor torque	n/a
Battery capacity	28kWh
Estimated range	80 miles
Max speed	75mph

GEM Car

The GEM car is probably the best kept secret of the US alternative motoring market. The thing is that many people think that the GEM is still a prototype. In reality, the manufacturer is currently owned by the DaimlerChrysler Corporation, and almost 50,000 units have been made since 1998. It is nothing more than a glorified golf cart, and being so simple and practical has ensured it enjoys steady demand. Currently, six versions of the GEM are being made – three passenger (two to six seats) and three commercial variations. There is nothing to be said about safety of a GEM car – the basic version doesn't even have the doors. However, it is officially a NEV, so it doesn't have to undergo a crash test. Apart from a strong USA dealer network, the GEM can be purchased in France, Germany, the Netherlands, Portugal, Spain, and Sweden. Not in the UK yet, though DaimlerChrysler plans to expand its GEM operation. The base price for a GEM two-seater is $7395. Fancy a pair of doors? Well that will cost you an extra $2000. Ah, wait, tarpaulin doors are two times cheaper! It may

A glorified golf cart called GEM – every gardener's dream. (Courtesy David Saunders)

sound funny but college campuses and parks love this little vehicle. OK, maybe people will stop smiling when GEM's new model – the PeaPod is finally released. It looks more like a car and is to be made from over 95 per cent recycled and recyclable materials.

Technical specifications
Motor power	9kW
Motor torque	n/a
Battery capacity	n/a
Estimated range	35 miles
Max speed	25mph

Kewet Buddy
The Buddy was born in 1991 in Denmark. Having undergone six major redesigns it has ended up in Norway – competing with the Th!nk car. Over the years, quite a few Buddys have been produced and sold. Today Elbil Norge AS (the current manufacturer of the car) plans to launch the Buddy in the rest of Europe. The Buddy is a compact and light three-seater, with a DC electric motor driving its rear wheels. Two under-floor battery pack options are available: lead and nickel metalhydride. These provide a range of 50 and 75 miles respectively. The Buddy's modest size allows for parallel parking. The base price is in the region of £16,000.

Yes, that's right. The founder, Jan Petter Skram, just had a ride in this white Buddy, and he's not a short man by any measure.
(Courtesy elbilnorge.no)

Investors explore the rugged tubular frame of a Buddy. It is constructed to be a safe car but the crash test results will tell.
(Courtesy Elbil Norge)

Technical specifications
Motor power	13kW
Motor torque	n/a
Battery capacity	various
Estimated range	75 miles
Max speed	50mph

Liberty Electric e-Range Rover
Being a Land Rover enthusiast, I obviously think that this is a good idea. The Oxford-based electric car start-up plans to retrofit Range Rover cars with an advanced electric drivetrain, and sell them for £100,000-125,000. The car would have a 200-mile range, and it would be the first luxury e-car in the world. Around £30 million has been invested in the company, and currently £1000 deposits are being taken for late 2010/early 2011 deliveries. If the Range Rover sells well, the company plans to introduce an electric Defender and a BMW Mini e-conversion in the near future.

Technical specifications
Motor power	n/a
Motor torque	n/a
Battery capacity	n/a
Estimated range	200 miles
Max speed	110mph

Lumeneo Smera

I don't really know what to make of the Lumeneo Smera. Although it's a four-wheel vehicle, it behaves like a motorbike, tilting during cornering by as much as 25 degrees. It's safe tilting, and the vehicle is designed to work that way. It is classified as a car (not a quad bike) in Europe, although it doesn't look like one.

The makers of Smera have estimated that, on average, a working person in France drives 13,800 kilometres (8600 miles) per year, spending 1070 Euros on fuel (as you can see fuel is cheaper in France but I don't think it comes as a huge surprise to you). Lumeneo says that driving a Smera, you'd spend only 97 Euros on electricity for the same amount of miles. Thus in ten years you'd save nearly 10,000 Euros. It is, of course, a nice little saving ... if the car wasn't so expensive. The tiny Smera, with a seating capacity for one adult, a child (or a dog), and a small bag, retails at 29,000 Euros. In France, as in many other countries, the Smera would qualify for a subsidy, but it still places it pricewise in line with five-seater sedans. You would expect that, for less motoring you'd get a lower price, but no – with electric cars it is vice versa.

Currently, the Lumeneo Smera is available only from a shop in Paris. Later this year the company plans to open shops in other European capitals. That's Smera's sales strategy – to sell the car from its own shops. No more dealerships and franchises. This is another way for small start-up car manufacturers to cut costs. Dealerships cost an enormous amount of money, and quite a chunk of the price you pay for a car will go towards that big shiny dealership pavilion and that smartly dressed young man who smirks at a few customers and does nothing for the rest of the day. For companies like

Lumeneo Smera is an ideal vehicle for those who can appreciate a car that feels like a bike. (Courtesy lumeneo.fr)

Smera, it makes more sense to rent a small shop and sell directly to the public. The company can justify the existence of each shop by selling only a dozen or so cars a year.

Technically, the Smera is rather advanced. Although it employs a simple direct belt transmission, everything in the vehicle is controlled by a computer. The data about speed and turning curves is digested to determine the right tilting angle. Although initially it might feel strange, Lumeneo promises easy handling and an amazing driving sensation. I bet the bikers will appreciate the tilting body right away.

Lumeneo is confident that its Li-ion battery would last ten years. This is the second time I've heard of a Li-ion battery lasting 100,000-plus miles, the first being Subaru's promise to guarantee its Li-ions for 124,000 miles.

Technical specifications

Motor power	30kW
Motor torque	1000Nm
Battery capacity	10kWh
Estimated range	90 miles
Max speed	80mph

Micro-Vett

Micro-Vett is the largest electric car producer in Italy. Although it would be capable of creating an original electric car, its business profile is to retrofit some of the most popular locally-produced cars with electric drivetrains. The Micro-Vett Porter is an electrified version of the Piaggio Porter micro-van. The Micro-Vett Daily is a full size electric delivery vehicle converted from the Iveco Daily. The biggest proportion of Micro-Vett's business is converting FIAT vehicles, both personal and commercial.

The e500 is an electric version of the FIAT 500 – another possible contender to hit high sales figures across Europe. Micro-Vett is expanding quickly. Its representatives are operating in France, Sweden, Norway, Czech Republic, Russia, and Ireland. A representative in the UK is currently being set up.

The e500 is a decent little car. It has all the safety and comfort features of a 'normal' FIAT, only it is electric.

Technical specifications

Motor power	30kW
Motor torque	n/a
Battery capacity	22kWh
Estimated range	90 miles
Max speed	70mph

Micro-Vett is the most important electric car manufacturer in Italy. This factory original Fiat e500 will compete with the unofficial Micro-Vett conversion very soon. (Courtesy FIAT)

Mitsubishi i MiEV, aka Peugeot iOn, aka Citroën C0

When first announced, the abbreviation MiEV stood for Mitsubishi In-wheel Motor Electric Vehicle, and several concept cars were presented based on the Colt and the Lancer with in-wheel motors. When, in 2006, the i MiEV (based on the petrol model i, whose name stood for innovation and immagination) was announced, everyone's first reaction was: "Hey, the first in-wheel model destined for production?" It turned out, though, that MiEV stood for Mitsubishi innovative Electric Vehicle this time; a little misleading. And after we add it to the initial i, what we get is … double innovation?

Mitsubishi is a fervent backer of in-wheel motor technology. It believes that placing the motors directly inside the wheel hubs is a great way to avoid using expensive transmissions and differentials. Apparently the company hasn't managed to balance out the unsprung weight of the wheels (read more about this in the Future Technology chapter) hence the production model i MiEV has a single electric motor on the rear axle.

The small 16kWh battery pack will take only six hours to charge from the 13A, 230V home outlet. It is also adapted for accepting fast charge. Currently, it seems that a large number of French on-street fast chargers have adopted a 125A, 400V scheme capable of putting 50kWh into batteries. At such a rate, an i MiEV battery could be charged in less than 20 minutes. In reality it'll take a little longer.

Although the motor is rather small and its torque level looks unimpressive, the i MiEV is an efficient car, and it consumes less power than an average electric car; only 0.16kWh per mile. This is one of the biggest advantages of the car. A major disadvantage, however, is

Although the i MiEV is obviously overpriced, many people are anticipating its arrival. (Courtesy Mitsubishi Motors)

the price. It will cost £39,000 in the UK, and will arrive in the showrooms at the beginning of 2011 to coincide with the £5000 Consumer Incentive Scheme. Even after the £5000 deduction, the car is hugely expensive. It's unlikely that many private buyers could stretch to £34,000 for a tiny four-seater that is no good for inter-city travel. It's expected that the i MiEV will be an instant hit with businesses that wouldn't fret about the price as long as they can claim first year capital allowance on it.

In France the car will be marketed as Citroën C0 or Peugeot iOn. It is more than probable that the French version of the i MiEV will start selling by the end of 2010.

Technical specifications
Motor power   47kW
Motor torque   180Nm
Battery capacity 16kWh
Estimated range 100 miles
Max speed   80mph

Modec
Although the Modec doesn't look big, its load capacity is quite impressive. Depending on the chassis it can take 11 to 15m3 of cargo weighing up to two tons. The van's gross weight is 5.5 tons, but that doesn't make it a low-range vehicle. In fact, its range is bang on 100 miles.

The company was established in 2004 in Coventry, England. It started producing vehicles in 2007 and, helped by an active interest from the Tesco supermarket chain, managed to sell 100 vans in the space of one year. The manufacturing unit in Coventry is theoretically capable of making 5000 vehicles a year. Unfortunately, the market is not capable of creating demand for such a large number of vehicles, though things are improving. Modec vans are a permanent feature in London, and thanks to a far-reaching dealer network branching out to the USA, the Netherlands, Spain, Germany, and other countries, the cars are beginning to establish themselves outside the UK as well.

Technical specifications
Motor power   85kW
Motor torque   300Nm
Battery capacity various
Estimated range 100 miles
Max speed   50mph

Spanish multi-service vehicle expert Ausa has modified this Modec to work in a recycling factory. (Courtesy Ausa Media, ausa.com)

Myers Motors NmG

Formerly known as the Corbin Sparrow, the car has a troubled past. Its original constructor went bankrupt in 2003, and, after a short hiatus, the Sparrow's intellectual property was bought by Dana Myers, who is now producing the funny little single-seater to order.

Myers describes his motivation to embark on such a treacherous business endeavour: "Myers Motors was founded to promote more global freedoms, such as the freedom to avoid incurring tens of billions of dollars of ill health effects in cities because of the pollutants primarily coming from car exhausts." According to MM America accounts for only five per cent of the global population but consumes 25 per cent of the world's energy. Myers wants to do something about it.

The car was also renamed from Sparrow to NmG, which means No More Gas. At the price tag of $29,995

it isn't a cheap car, but that hasn't stopped Myers Motors receiving orders. There are people who are really keen on the wacky little three-wheeler.

Nevertheless, the company is betting its future on what seems to be a better buy: the Myers Motors Duo. Although, it being a two-seater, you might think that 'Duo' has something to do with the number of seats; it doesn't. Duo stands for 'Doesn't Use Oil.' Myers tells it as it is. He needs at least 1000 pre-orders to be able to produce the Duo to reach the volume pricing. The original price tag is the same as the NmG – $29,995 – but there's a $5000 discount for the first 1000 orders, bringing the price down to $24,995, and, as Myers rightly notes, the car is eligible for the US Federal tax credit of ten per cent (a further $2499 off). With a final price of $22,495 it doesn't seem so ridiculous. The base price is for a car with a 60-mile range. To extend it to 80

Formerly known as Sparrow, the little runabout is resurrected under the management of Myers Motors. (Courtesy myersmotors.com)

miles, with a battery pack boost, you'll need to part with another $2500.

The MM cars always grab the attention of other motorists. They are quirky and flashy, clearly stating the fact that they're environmentally friendly cars (something companies like Ford strongly oppose, regarding this as a private matter). It's good that the cars are so different and fit for different kinds of people.

Both Myers Motors models have a practical boot space that, according to the maker, is large enough to accommodate the contents of a shopping trolley. MM has set a target of reaching 1000 pre-orders for the Duo by the time this book goes to print; let's hope it succeeds.

Technical specifications (NmG)

Motor power	20kW
Motor torque	n/a
Battery capacity	6.2kWh
Estimated range	45 miles
Max speed	75mph

Technical specifications (Duo)

Motor power	n/a
Motor torque	n/a
Battery capacity	n/a
Estimated range	60-100 miles
Max speed	n/a

NICE Mega City & Multitruck Van

Mega City isn't a reference to *The Matrix* or *Judge Dredd*. Mega is a French car maker popular for its golf buggies and licence-free microcars. Decades of experience with small cars had to produce an electric car sooner or later.

When it comes to microcars, Europe is a territory of many official standards. In countries like France, Italy, Portugal, and a few others, you can drive a Mega without a driving licence if you're at least 16 years old. Isn't it

It is a NICE car – stylish and economical. (Courtesy mega-vehicles.com)

The fantastic boot space makes the car attractive for pizza delivery services, too. (Courtesy Mega Vehicles)

funny? You make a car so small that it doesn't qualify as a car any more and then it suddenly becomes safe for teenagers to drive!

Mega City is registered as a quad bike, just like the REVA G-Wiz. And just like its Indian competitor, the City doesn't have to undergo an official crash test. However, if it did, it would fare better than the Reva, simply because it is bigger and it has a superior build quality.

Mega Multitruck – see the smile on the driver's face? There's plenty to smile about if you're in business – this car would be eligible for a 100 per cent tax credit. (Courtesy Mega Vehicles)

Mega electric cars are imported into Britain by a company called NICE. The two-seater is rather comfortable, and has a huge cargo compartment. Almost 30ft³ of cargo space makes it a good small delivery vehicle. The prices start from £12,500. This isn't cheap for a car that is equipped with basic lead-acid batteries. Not that the lack of Li-ion technology onboard makes any difference in the range of the vehicle; it's on a par with other limited-speed NEVs.

Although pizza delivery companies are generally happy with the Mega City, there is a larger option. A 50-mile range van called Multitruck starts at £12,000 plus VAT. It also comes with a refrigerator as an option. The same lead-acid battery technology is used, hence the relatively reasonable price.

Technical specifications (City)

Motor power	4.5kW
Motor torque	n/a
Battery capacity	n/a
Estimated range	60 miles
Max speed	40mph

Nissan Leaf

Many experts predict that the Leaf will quickly become one of the top-selling electric cars in the world. Although the Renault-Nissan alliance has done a great job in developing electric cars fit for mass-scale production, it sometimes seems that it's the clever public awareness campaign that has placed the Leaf in the position of being one of the world's most popular electric cars, even before its assembly has begun.

There were rumours that Nissan would start taking deposits for the Leaf electric car in spring 2010. The first electric cars would reach drivers in the USA by December 2010. However, at the end of the spring there was still no sign of pre-reservations; only the newsletter sign-up form was functioning.

It's been estimated that almost 50,000 Americans have signed up for updates on the Leaf project. I don't expect that all of them would jump at the opportunity to buy the Leaf, but it is more than certain that the order book will contain tens of thousands of names. It will be the largest Ecar campaign in the western world to date, and several US energy companies are unveiling their plans for improving the infrastructure so that the drivers can top-up their cars in parking lots and other public spaces.

Nissan had kept the price secret until recently when it was revealed that the car would retail in the USA for $32,780. After the federal tax break it drops to $25,280, and residents of California and Georgia would enjoy a further $5000 state rebate making the Leaf cost just a little over $20,000; now that's a reasonable price. Nissan doesn't expect to make much money out of its American campaign. The true cost of the Nissan Leaf can be estimated by looking at the company's

Nissan Leaf – another full-size family five-seater that would have no problem passing a safety test. (Courtesy Nissan Motors)

local price list. The Leaf in Japan would cost over $40,000.

Initially it was expected that the price would not include batteries (instead, they would be available on lease). As it currently stands, however, it seems that the batteries will be included.

The European price of the Leaf is still unknown. Nissan definitely wants to conquer Europe, and Britain will be at the very centre of the campaign. Not much to cheer about, though. In the UK the retail price will be £28,350 (approximately $42,750) and that is for the car that, according to the press release, is to be assembled in Sunderland. You'd certainly anticipate it to cost less here ...

What's good about Nissan's Leaf is that it's a five-seat, proper-size family car, and it will, hopefully, have no problem with European crash tests. There's nothing revolutionary in the car, but the time that Nissan has spent on creating and fine-tuning the 'Nissan EV Platform' ensures that all future cars

Don't be surprised to find a charging outlet in the most unusual places – it's a whole new world. (Courtesy Nissan Motors)

based on this platform will have the best available technology on-board.

Nissan's new dedicated EV platform will serve as a focal point for its future electric car range. The platform is full-size car oriented (no more eggshell single-seaters) and it provides improved safety with a highly rigid body concept. An additional frame improves the rigidity and helps eliminate vibration. The platform features an updated regenerative braking system, and a sophisticated IT system connects each electric car and charging station into an interactive global web. This system will allow you to see your current available driving radius (according to the battery level) on a convenient navigation map. You will also see the available charging stations. All these improvements sound really good, but, alas, they won't increase the vehicle's range over 100 miles.

Still, the Nissan Leaf is definitely the one to watch. It won't make you choose between the comfort you're used to and the environment, but it can potentially make both sides happy.

Technical specifications

Motor power	80kW
Motor torque	280Nm
Battery capacity	24kWh
Estimated range	100 miles
Max speed	90mph

Optimal Energy Joule

Around 2008, when the South African Joule made its debut in Paris, I was given so much contradictory information on the car that I really didn't know what to make of it. One thing was certain though: it was beautiful, and, befitting the company's name, optimal in size. Designed by South African Keith Helfet, and prototyped by the famous Italian studio Zagato, it made a very good impression. In its initial form, the

Joule was a six-seater (two rows by three like the FIAT Multipla) with an unidentified powertrain configuration. The company was still playing with different concepts, the most interesting of all being four separate electric motors for each wheel. The rumours leaked in the Asian media suggested that the car would use Chinese batteries, be ready by 2010, and that production would reach 4000 cars per year. No-one paid much attention to those rumours, and rightfully so (especially knowing that the SA infrastructure couldn't bear the extra load of a newly sprung fleet of electric cars). Two years on and the Joule is back. The batteries, apparently, will be made locally, which is always a good thing, and there's a more realistic production date – 2013.

However, several test cars are due to run during the Football World Cup in June, 2010. The current take on creating an 'optimal' electric car is a five-seater with a single 75kW electric motor. The battery pack provides 36kWh of energy, which seems enough to cover more than 140 miles on one charge. The engineers at Optimal Energy are considering putting solar batteries on the roof, thus increasing the range even further. The car promises to be pretty easy to drive

The South African take on the electric car idea; visually very appealing.
(Courtesy optimalenergy.com)

– it has a single speed transmission, so forget about switching gears. Although many companies are trying to develop a transmission especially for electric cars, at the moment it seems a wiser decision to stick to a single-speed transmission because electric motors provide almost constant torque regardless of the revolutions.

Optimal Energy is a young company (started in 2005) and serves as proof that you don't need to be a large establishment to come up with a competitive new car.

Although it will probably be 2014 or 2015 before the Joule arrives in Europe, this car is definitely one to watch, and I bet many manufacturers will try to pinch an idea or two from the great package it presents. The Joule is a proper-size family car that doesn't compromise on safety. It's pretty close to what a future electric car might look like.

Safety comes first in this electric SUV. (Courtesy phoenixmotorcars.com)

Another version of the Phoenix for pick-up lovers. (Courtesy Phoenix Motorcars)

Technical specifications
Motor power   75kW
Motor torque   280Nm
Battery capacity   35kWh
Estimated range   143 miles
Max speed   84mph

Phoenix SUV
The American electric car company Phoenix Motorcars takes a very reasonable approach to alternative motoring. It's developing two full-size models based on the popular Ssang Yong Actyon: a sports utility vehicle (SUV) for private owners, and a light truck for businesses. Although the cars weigh more than two tons, they have the same range of 100 miles – an average for a modern electric car. According to the company, its main advantage is a fast-charging option. Thanks to AltairNano's lithium-titanate battery and a specially designed high-power charging system (250kW instead

of the 3kW you're getting out of your plug) it will be possible to charge the car in some ten to 15 minutes. The high-power charging system will work only where the grid can handle high loads. The home outlet of an average American (or European) just won't cut it. If nothing else, the Phoenix SUV is a very safe vehicle.

Phoenix Motorcars has found that in California alone the commercial sector for light vehicles and trucks (for businesses, municipalities, etc.) is worth $10 billion a year, with over 200,000 vehicles sold. The company wants a share of it in 2011, with plans to expand outside the USA within the next couple of years.

Technical specifications
Motor power   110kW
Motor torque   500Nm
Battery capacity   35kWh
Estimated range   100 miles
Max speed   95mph

The complete range of Renault's electric car expansion plan. From left-to-right: Fluence, Twizy, Kangoo Z.E., and Zoe. (Courtesy Renault, photo by P Curtet)

Renault Z.E.

Z.E. (Zero Emission) is the codename of the large-scale electric car campaign by Renault. It includes four models: Fluence, Twizy, Kangoo Z.E., and Zoe. So far, the Z.E. range is probably the most serious attempt in the emerging electric car market by any European car manufacturer.

Renault is a great believer in electric cars. It once estimated that by 2020 at least ten per cent of all new cars sold would be electric vehicles. That might be a little optimistic, considering that the large car manufacturers will have had only nine full seasons of selling electric cars by 2020. Just like many of its competitors, Renault will launch its first electric car, the Kangoo Express Z.E., in the summer of 2011. Soon after, the quirky, single-seater electropod Twizy will appear. The launch of the long-awaited family car Fluence Z.E. has been deferred to 2012, and will probably coincide with the debut of the Zoe sports coupé. These four models will provide Renault with a presence in almost every profitable niche of the automotive market.

Unlike other manufacturers concentrating solely on California or their own local markets, Renault will be ready to offer its electric cars across the world, particularly in Eastern Europe.

The Renault-Nissan alliance has spent over $5 billion on developing electric cars and battery technology. To cut the costs and the grey energy that goes into producing the cars, it will produce batteries in France, the UK, the USA, and Japan. The Kangoo will be made in France, but when the Fluence comes about, it will most likely be outsourced to Turkey.

It is not a coincidence that the Kangoo hits the market first: Renault is targeting companies that can claim their capital allowances. The first couple of years of electric car sales to the private sector will be extremely slow; and by launching a commercial model first, Renault would have a chance to see if it can sustain the production volume required to make a profit. There's no reason why businesses would not want to give the Kangoo Z.E. a go. It'll have the same cargo volume as the conventional Kangoo, and, with a 100 per cent first year capital allowance (may be different in countries other than the UK), the choice between an electric Kangoo and a diesel one is a no-brainer.

The Fluence X-ray showing off the car's safety features. Note the 'dented' profile above the front wheel – a very clever way of executing a shock-absorbing element. (Courtesy Renault)

The plan is to introduce photovoltaic panel roofs and LED-based lights to save energy and increase the range even further.

Renault also wants to explore the option of fast 'refuelling.' In its opinion, the best solution would be slot-in batteries. This means that empty batteries could be replaced with charged ones in less than three minutes. A strong network of special battery exchange stations will have to be created within cities to make this option viable. One can hardly begin to imagine how expensive that would be? According to Renault, any sort of fast-charge facilities will become viable not earlier than in 2013. There is a technology that allows a Kangoo to be fully recharged in less than 30 minutes.

The Fluence will be the key factor in Renault's electric car strategy. (Courtesy Renault)

Technical specifications (Kangoo)

Motor power	44kW
Motor torque	226Nm
Battery capacity	15kWh
Estimated range	100 miles
Max speed	80mph

Technical specifications (Fluence)

Motor power	70kW
Motor torque	226Nm
Battery capacity	22kWh
Estimated range	100 miles
Max speed	84mph

REVA G-Wiz

At first I didn't want to include this vehicle in the model catalogue, but as there are so many driving around in London, and in case you might be wondering ... well, here goes.

The REVA is not a car – and I'm not saying this to insult the people who spent seven years painstakingly developing it. It doesn't have to be registered as a car. Technically, it's a quad bike with a rigid body and you may drive it on a licence that allows you to drive any quad bike. The reason why it's classed as a quad bike is so the Indian manufacturer can sell the vehicles in England without undergoing crash tests. If it had to go through a proper crash test, the REVA would fail. There have been several unofficial crash tests involving the REVA, and the results show that it is not a very safe car. A little while ago, the UK Vehicle Certification Agency performed a 35mph crash test of the G-Wiz that proved high risk of injury for occupants. As a result, the Department for Transport claimed it was reviewing the safety requirements for quad bikes. Obviously, they are still under review because more and more REVAs are being sold.

The REVA is not a particularly good-looking car; it certainly lags behind the standards of modern European design. But then, why should we complain if the design was clearly derived from a little-known French car (the Erad Agora, developed from the mid-1980s to 1993 by the Society of Automotive Studies and Projects of Douaisis). The REVA is also not very cheap for a quad bike (with prices in the UK starting at £8995), but we would be more forgiving of its faults if it were safer. The idea is brilliant – a small car for a big city, easy to manoeuvre and easy to park.

You might be relatively safe driving a REVA in cities like London where

REVA G-Wiz – according to Aerosmith, apparently falling in love with small electric cars is "hard on your knees."
(Courtesy Frank Hebbert, released on a Creative Commons Licence)

traffic is pleasantly docile and slow. However, anywhere with the potential for frontal collision comes with a risk. And even in slow traffic, the car is so narrow that if somebody were to hit you in the side, you would have a nasty bump on your head, plus some bruises. A slow-speed frontal collision would probably result in injured knees if you're five feet or over. The REVA Electric Car Company says that during the nine years the REVA has been produced, there have been no fatalities or serious injuries. Well, how many fatalities occur in the centre of London? All vehicles driven on public roads, be it the slow heart of London or a hyper-fast German autobahn, should be constructed with passenger safety in mind. No exceptions! At Volvo in its golden years, for example, one of the first things a development team did on a new model was calculate the potential energy of an impact, how many crunch zones the car needed, how would the material absorb the impact ... That's the only proper way of building cars.

The REVA safety compromise is a huge pity because it was designed with safety in mind. The tubular steel frame, side impact beams and bumpers with energy absorbent crush cones (the bumper is attached to the body via energy absorbent elements) make it potentially safe. Its main fault is the width of the interior ... OK, actually all the car's dimensions are one big problem. All the injuries that a driver or passengers might suffer will probably be self-inflicted by bumping heads at the pillars and windows and hurting the knees at the dashboard. Can they make REVA a bit bigger?

There is a new REVA on the horizon, called NXR and meant for intercity driving. Intercity suggests that it will be a car ready for speeding down a highway. Judging by its dimensions, it might struggle to meet the Euro NCAP (a car safety performance assessment programme devised in European Union) rigorous safety standards.

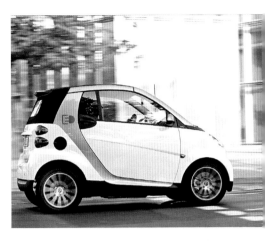

It's a smart move – this car has proven itself as a conventional vehicle and there's no reason why it couldn't be successful as an electric vehicle. After years of development one would expect it to sail through any crash tests. (Courtesy Smart Cars)

Technical specifications

Motor power	13kW
Motor torque	68Nm
Battery capacity	9.6kWh
Estimated range	40 miles
Max speed	40mph

smart ED (AKA smart EV)

The DaimlerChrysler Corporation has been working on an electric smart for a while. The last two years have seen several field tests of the new car, and trials have been carried out involving council and police forces in several places across the UK. The company is in no hurry to launch the ED. Although the test results are encouraging, the smart ED won't go on the production lines before 2012.

The smart ED is an international project. After Tesla Motors sold nine per cent share stake to DaimlerChrysler, it became clear that the two companies might consider a joint project. It was estimated that Daimler parted with

$50 million to acquire a seat on Tesla's director board. It seems that Tesla Motors will be developing smart's power system, including the batteries. The high-tech electric motor is provided by British company Zytek – that's one of the reasons why so many field tests are carried out in Britain.

smart cars (along with the Daewoo Matiz) are the most copied mini-car designs in the world. Many Chinese made smart-look-alikes (and Matiz-based three-wheelers) are entering the US market as NEVs without safety tests and homologation. If it looks like a smart but doesn't have the smart badge and specifications: just follow your common sense ...

Technical specifications

Motor power	30kW
Motor torque	120Nm
Battery capacity	14kWh
Estimated range	84 miles
Max speed	62mph

Smith Electric Newton

Anyone who remembers the early Co-op milk floats in the UK must be familiar with the name Smith Electric. The company built the first milk floats in 1920, but by the early 2000s was facing bankruptcy. However, the electric delivery truck Newton, launched in 2006, put the company back on its feet, and within the space of a few years it has grown to become the world's largest electric vehicle manufacturer. The Newton has been a roaring success, with the Sainsbury's supermarket chain, alone, running almost 1000. DHL, TNT and Royal Mail are among the many other UK companies known to run Newtons. The Newton, in its jumbo-12-ton-version, which reaches 9.1 metres in length, is the largest street-legal electric vehicle on the planet.

Currently owned by the Tyneside based Tanfield Group, Smith Electric is one of the last big British companies not yet sold to foreign investors to please the shareholders.

The Newton is an ideal delivery truck for companies based in large towns. It blends in with the traffic very well, and, compared with a similar 12-ton diesel vehicle, accelerates quicker and causes less aggravation to other road users.

Several battery pack options are available. With the most advanced Li-ion battery the Newton takes just six to eight hours to recharge. This means that it can do two shifts in a day covering as much as 300 miles in total.

Tanfield has recently acquired a plant in Kansas, USA, which, although manned by just 40 employees, manages to build five to ten vehicles a week. Last October, when there were only 14 people working at the plant (plus five experts from the UK) they built 12 vehicles from scratch. The eventual goal is to produce 25 Newtons per week by the end of 2010. After the partnership with Ford Motors to build Transit Connect pick-ups fell through, it seemed that Smith's US operation was doomed, but it admits that it never intended to concentrate on small commercial vehicles. As a result the company decided to do its own thing by producing large-size electric trucks.

All this would probably be more difficult if Smith didn't have a helping hand from the locals. The US Department of Energy assigned a $10 million grant to Smith, plus it received a $3 million tax credit from the Missouri government.

Apart from the jumbo Newton, Smith also makes the Edison Van, which in essence is a converted Ford Transit (don't confuse this with the Transit Connect) providing for a payload of up to 1.2 tons in a panel van version.

Technical specifications

Motor power	120kW
Motor torque	n/a
Battery capacity	various
Estimated range	150 miles
Max speed	50mph

Smith Electric Newton – Brits are taking the USA by storm. The Newton is establishing itself as the world's best selling electric truck. (Courtesy Smith Electric, smithelectricvehicles.com)

Shelby means speed, regardless of how you look at it. The SSC Ultimate Aero – easily the world's fastest electric vehicle, that is if you forget the Japanese trains. (Courtesy SSC, shelbysupercars.com)

SSC Ultimate Aero EV

Jerod Shelby, no relation to Carroll Shelby, is a product design engineer, and this supercar is the manifestation of his unsinkable enthusiasm for exotic cars. After finishing his kart racing career, Jerod switched to building Ferrari and Lamborghini replicas. The hobby grew into a full-scale endeavour when he built the SSC (Shelby Super Cars) Ultimate Aero supercar. In 2007 it achieved a top speed of 256mph, had a 6.2-litre, 1183bhp monster engine, and environmentalists hated it! Then, however, Jerod Shelby came up with a new idea – to produce an electric supercar.

It won't be cheap. The petrol versions of the SSC Ultimate Aero are selling for $430,000-$480,000, and there's no reason to think that the electric version would be any cheaper. Of course, it's not the most expensive supercar in the world. And besides, if you're considering buying a supercar, the price shouldn't be the most

important element in your equation.

Shelby claims that in the near future his All-Electric Scalable Powertrain (AESP) will be produced in different sizes pertaining to different applications. The smallest drivetrain with a 149kW power will be good for small delivery trucks, while the high-end 894kW monster will appeal to the Ministry of Defence and other organizations looking for ultimate power.

Unlike other cars, the SSC Ultimate Aero EV has a three-speed automatic transmission. It cannot live with just a reduction gear. Something needs to take control of the double-motor drivetrain with a total power exceeding 745kW (1000bhp).

The SSC Ultimate Aero EV is a good-looking car; 100 per cent American; you'll know it when you see one (though you'd be lucky as they're very thin on the ground). Although it was announced that the production of SSC Ultimate Aero Electric would start late in 2009, no electric car has yet been delivered. When it eventually hits production, though, it'll knock the Tesla Roadster from its pedestal of the fastest production electric car in the world.

Technical specifications

Motor power	745kW
Motor torque	1083Nm
Battery capacity	n/a
Estimated range	150 miles
Max speed	208mph

Stevens Zecar

Developed by father and son team Professor Tony Stevens (once a chief designer for Rootes), and his son Peter (an ex-City banker), the Zecar is a family five-seater. It's a quirky little car, built to comply with both UK and international vehicle construction standards, and it can go anywhere apart from highways and those roads where the speed limit is higher than 50mph. The Stevens are producing the cars at the Engineering Centre for Manufacturing and Materials (ECM²).

The Zecar and its commercial brother the Zevan have been developed as safe vehicles (even though the Stevens have determined that almost 75 per cent of British motorists do less than ten miles a day, and the average traffic speed in London is only 12mph). Although no crash tests have yet been performed, the company has run a virtual safety test in the UK Transport Research Laboratory and the results looked good. The car is designed around a steel safety cage incorporating the much important crunch zones and chassis joints that absorb crash impact energy.

ZeCar by Stevens Vehicles. This British-made model could become a contender. The projected retail price is around £20,000. (Courtesy Stevens Vehicles, stevensvehicles.co.uk)

Peter Stevens with a ZeVan – the commercial version of Stevens' electric vehicle. (Courtesy Stevens Vehicles)

Stevens has developed an ultra-low carbon emission manufacturing process. The whole building cycle releases 4500kg of CO_2. It may sound a lot, but it's actually three times lower than a conventional car that creates 15,000kg of greenhouse gases even before it hits the street. Only Twike has a better result (from companies which have publicized their grey energy ratios) – currently 3600kg – but then this is a velomobile and the Stevens Zecar is a family five-seater.

Once mass-scale production is established, the company plans to expand worldwide by building small factories around the world, especially in rural locations. That sort of production method would be great for deprived regions as it would create jobs where it is most needed, but a decentralized chain of small factories incur transport expenses and, alas, more grey energy because shifting parts and equipment around the world is still a very carbon-intensive procedure. However, with a grey energy level currently at 4500kg, Stevens can afford to add a bit more for the sake of a regional economic boost.

A few cars are known to have been built to order in Port Talbot, Wales. Large-scale production is something that will require a much larger financial commitment, but the Stevens are determined. Although supported by the Welsh Assembly government, it will take some time for the company to gain momentum. It is also developing a new hydrogen-free fuel cell system, and is working on other innovations (including a bio-diesel hybrid). In the hybrid execution, the Zecar can do 30 miles on batteries, and then a further 100 miles on a full bio-diesel tank. The problem, though, is that, in the UK at least, petrol stations with bio-diesel supply are few and far between.

Technical specifications

Motor power	52kW
Motor torque	216Nm
Battery capacity	10-20kWh
Estimated range	50-100 miles
Max speed	56mph

Subaru Stella EV

Japan is serious about electric cars. Late in 2009 the first experimental high-speed charging points were unveiled by the Kanagawa District Governor Shigefumi Matsuzawa. This high-speed charger takes just 15 to 30 minutes to fill the Li-ion batteries to 80 per cent charge level, depending on the electric car model. Similar chargers have also been installed near the Metropolitan and the Hanshin expressways. More parking places will be equipped with charging points in 2010 and the following years.

The problem with the Japan's new fast-charge system, however, is that very few electric cars can accept it. It's likely that the new system employs high voltages, and the majority of the electric cars available now would just start 'boiling their batteries.' The Subaru

Subaru Stella – according to the Japanese manufacturer, this car's Li-ion batteries could last for up to ten years.
(Courtesy Subaru Motors)

Stella EV is one car that will be able to accept fast-charging. It is built so that a 15-minute stint at the Hanshin expressway charging plot will enable it to cover another 50 miles. This is no coincidence: Subaru's electric car models are being developed in collaboration with Tokyo Electric Power – the company behind installation of the fast-charge points. Just like Ford and some other manufacturers, Subaru has chosen to convert two of its popular city cars, instead of building a brand new car especially for its electric drivetrain. This is how large manufacturers cut costs and try to keep the retail price of their electric cars as low as possible.

Along with the Stella family microvan, Subaru is developing a 2+2 city car – the R1e.

Subaru is one of the few companies revealing what it thinks about Li-ion battery life. With the Subaru R1e, it's thought that the batteries could last up to 124,000 miles, or ten years; not bad if it's really true. Subaru is so confident about its electric drivetrain that it is considering licensing the technology to other car makers.

Both the Subaru Stella EV and the R1e are currently developed for the local market, but surely the company has its sights set on Europe and the rest of the world, too? Now that Toyota and Mitsubishi have green automotive technology available for the western market, there's no way Subaru will want to remain aloof.

As a test model the Stella is some way from being perfect, and technical specifications are not very impressive. There is room for improvement, and that room, I dare say, will be filled to the ceiling. Also, the price will be pretty high – estimated at $48,000 (according to Edmund's *Automotive News* aggregator). Currently, though, the Stella is being tested by local government

services and, so far, councillors and agents are pretty happy with how the car behaves. According to the Spanish Institute for Diversity in Energy, the Stella might arrive in Europe as early as the last quarter of 2010. I think this might be a little optimistic, and I doubt that the Stella will make it in time for the UK's electric car incentive.

Technical specifications (Stella)

Motor power	47kW
Motor torque	170Nm
Battery capacity	n/a
Estimated range	56 miles
Max speed	63mph

Tango

It might take two to tango, but it'll certainly take more than two to roll over this thing. Narrow as it is, the Tango has been constructed so that it doesn't end up on its roof. It's a weird little car, but actor George Clooney thinks it's good (he was the first person outside the factory circle to take delivery of a Tango).

At just 39 inches wide (that's less than a metre!) you can park it sideways, or even two of them side-by-side in a normal parking space. However, although small, the car actually weighs more than 1.3 tons. The majority of the weight is under the floor, courtesy of batteries and two DC motors, each powering a rear wheel; that's why it's so hard to roll over a Tango. This little vehicle gives you everything you'd expect from a motorbike (brilliant acceleration, high top speed), but it's much safer.

A major drawback for the Tango is its high price. Clooney's car (the model T600) cost $121,000 and, while that's acceptable for Hollywood folk, it's no good for the average speed-freak. Commuter Cars, the company behind the Tango, is developing a

The Tango two-seater. It's George Clooney's favourite, but then the actor doesn't have to fret too much about budget.
(Courtesy Commuter Cars, commutercars.com)

Elise's famous cousin – it is probably the most talked-about car of the 2009. Let's see if it lives up to its reputation.
(Courtesy Tesla Motors, teslamotors.com)

simpler variant, though, the Tango T200, which will apparently cost around $40,000 as a bare kit for DIY assembly; batteries not included. The cheapest lead-acid batteries will cost an extra $4000, whereas the high-spec Li-ion batteries with a ten year warranty will be $25,000. It's certainly a unique vehicle, and you can't expect a small company to develop a production car at a reasonable price, but if a similar car would have been created in Asia, it would probably cost in the region of $8000 (that's an estimate I got from comparing some of the most popular Chinese electric cars). And that's where the Western companies are losing out. They never seem to manage to get their act together before they are bought out by somebody who will transfer all the jobs to Asia and make the prices really low.

Technical specifications

Motor power	198kW
Motor torque	1400Nm
Battery capacity	n/a
Estimated range	80 miles
Max speed	135mph

Tesla Roadster

The Tesla Roadster is currently the only highway-capable, mass-produced electric car. The remaining are either NEVs or, like Nissans, Renaults, Minis, and others, although having been produced in the hundreds, in reality still only testing prototypes.

Tesla is a new kind of car manufacturer. It's corporate personality very far from the traditional Detroit values. Based in California, in so-called 'Silicon Valley,' it really feels like one of those hi-tech companies that make strange gadgets whose name you cannot pronounce. The self-made multimillionaire Elon Musk, co-founder and key financier of Tesla, made his fortune on the internet before the dot-com bubble burst. He is also the co-founder of PayPal – the internet payments system.

The Tesla Roadster made its debut in 2006 after three long years in the making. Initially based on AC Propulsion's Tzero, the Roadster later lost all its AC-licenced components in favour of Tesla's own know-how.

The Tesla Roadster seemingly has only two downsides. One is the price, and the other one is logistics. Just like

Mini E, the Roadster is pre-assembled, dis-assembled, and then re-assembled in different parts of the world. The chassis is made in Britain by Lotus using components shipped in from the USA, Germany, and France. The half-ready cars then travel across the globe to California for the drivetrain assembly. I am aware that all high-quality cars will have components from the leading European manufacturers, but shipping the chassis to and fro around the world accrues a lot of grey energy.

The US base price for the Roadster is $109,000, and the car is eligible for the federal tax incentive ($7500), but that still doesn't make it cheap (though it was never intended to be). Considering that the body panels are made entirely from carbon fibre composite, it's a cheap car in its category. In order to make a similar composite car body in a traditional way (manually – as some of the independent car makers do), it would cost nearly as much as the whole Roadster. Tesla's designers have devised a clever method that allows them to achieve the same quality at a fraction of the cost. In the UK the base price will be around £86,000, whereas on the continent it will cost 84,000 Euros. Somehow, it seems, the Brits always end up paying more, which is ridiculous and unfair considering that the majority of the work on the production cars is done in the UK.

The first right-hand drive vehicles have already been supplied, but, in the UK, those sold after 1st January 2011 will be eligible for £5000 cash back. Road tax and the London congestion

The interior fits the bill – Tesla Roadster looks expensive inside and out. (Courtesy Tesla Motors)

charge will be waived, saving another couple of thousand. It will also be exempt from the Showroom Tax; so another thousand saved. In London there are free parking spaces and free charging top-up points for electric cars, and then there's savings on 'fuel.' 'Savings' and 'sports cars' doesn't really fit well within one sentence, does it? Well, actually, Tesla Roadster is a very efficient and low-operation-cost sports car and, after all the cash-backs and perks, you're looking at a £10,000 saving in the first year, and £5000 a year from then on (compared to all other £80,000-range sports cars). But then, if you're considering a Tesla Roadster, I doubt you're too bothered about saving money.

The Tesla Roadster is currently being built to order, and so far more than 1000 cars have been produced. Most of the reviews and feedback are positive, and it looks like the estimated range of 200 miles per charge is realistic. Although there are people who challenge the claims, some reports suggest that the car is capable of more if driven carefully. Allegedly the record was set in late 2009 when a car went more than 300 miles on a single charge.

In case you're wondering what the rear-wheel-drive Roadster is like, think Lotus Elise – both models share some parts and equipment, and, initially, the Roadster was based on the Elise. At one stage in development the platform of the two cars was identical. Currently, though, Tesla has moved on, and the majority of it is original. However, the wheelbase of the Tesla is only two inches longer than that of the Elise, so, they are certainly within the same segment. If you like the Lotus Elise, you should be content with the Roadster as well. It's three times more expensive than the Elise, but if you can appreciate the high technology and all-carbon-fibre body, it should be a nice buy.

Fot those who can't or don't want to purchase the Roadster, there is an option to lease it. You get an initial three-year fixed mileage (30,000) lease after making a $10,000 downpayment. The monthly payment is $1658.

Technical specifications

Motor power	215kW
Motor torque	370Nm
Battery capacity	53kWh
Estimated range	200 miles
Max speed	125mph

Tesla Model S

The Model S is a luxury five-seater sedan concept developed by Tesla. It made its official debut in 2009, and is set to appear on the market in 2012. With the new car Tesla knows that it has to target the less affluent sector of the public in order to expand beyond being a niche 'toy-maker.' The base price of the Model S will be in the region of $57,400, placing it in the same 'showroom' as the BMW 5 and the Mercedes Benz E. Will the Model S cut it?

The Model S promises to be a worthy, multimedia-packed car, with a permanent internet connection and 3G mobile.

The concept was created by Henrik Fisker who, after a scandal, moved on to start his own company and now develops the Fisker Karma – a clear competitor to the Model S.

Currently, the Tesla Model S is available to pre-order, and it's known that a couple of thousand applications have been received. Considering that the deposit for the Model S stands at $5000, the company has already accumulated a few million dollars. It looks like the electric sedan is reasonably priced for the segment it would cater for.

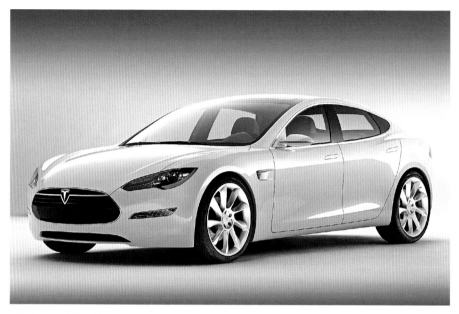

Tesla Model S – this sleek family car is said to be the future of motoring. (Courtesy Tesla Motors)

Performance is expected to be spot on for competing with German imports. Zero to 60mph will take 5.6 seconds, and maximum speed will be 120mph. Despite having a nice streamlined body, the drag coefficient is 0.28, which is rather high for a car that wants to be as efficient as possible (although well within the average for five-seater sedans, I believe there's room for improvement). When it comes to aerodynamics, there are certain limitations to what a designer can do in order to achieve both an optimal drag coefficient and an appealing body design. A milestone for green car design, in my opinion, is the Solectria Sunrise whose drag coefficient was 0.17.

Range-wise Tesla's designers are aiming at 300 miles with the largest Li-ion battery pack. They're also working on a fast-charge system that would quick-charge the battery in 45 minutes using a high-voltage (non-domestic) outlet.

Technical specifications

Motor power	215kW
Motor torque	n/a
Battery capacity	85kWh
Estimated range	300 miles
Max speed	120mph

Th!nk City

This is probably one of the best-researched electric cars in the world – and the longest in development. The small Norwegian company began in 1991 under the name of PIVco (Personal Independent Vehicle Company), and in just three years presented a small fleet of working prototypes well in time for the Lillehammer Olympic Games. The current Th!nk City is based on the PIV4 prototype developed together with Lotus. As finances dried up, the Norwegian company was acquired by Ford, which subsequently lost interest in the project and sold it on to KamKorp –

Th!nk City trying an inter-city outing. With an estimated range of just over 100 miles, it can do it ... (Photo by Knut Bry, Courtesy of Th!nk, think.no)

a Pakistani-Swiss company. The original owner, Jan Otto Ringdal, then regained control of his dormant brainchild in 2006, and things have gone uphill since then. Th!nk city has gone out of the development phase and is now a real production car, on sale in Norway and Austria. During 2010 the Th!nk will, hopefully, become available across other Scandinavian countries and in Spain. What about Britain? Well, the company promised that the 'City' would arrive in Britain in 2009. That didn't happen. The next target is early 2011, and considering the £5000 subsidy it would be really silly of the Norwegian company not to make its car available to Britain on time. As for America, despite having tested the cars in California and New York during Ford ownership, there's no real deadline set for Th!nk to conquer the States. It's generally known that Mr Ringdal is interested in the USA market, but it might be another couple of years before his car makes it across the ocean.

Technically, Th!nk is a result of 20 years of research and trial-and-error. Compared with some newly-developed electric cars, this might give it an edge. The Norwegians have adopted a very unusual philosophy for the industrial

world. They talk about a holistic approach – an idea which is more common in non-orthodox medicine and alternative lifestyles. A holistic approach means that a system or organism cannot be reduced down to components to explain how it functions. Instead, the system or organism (the car in this instance) should be treated as a whole. What it means for the Th!nk is that the whole process of sourcing the materials and working out the technological process is orientated towards sustainability. Ironically, the company won't be able to maintain this holistic approach when it comes to the batteries. It's not possible to source lithium in Norway, and the company that produces the batteries for Th!nk (A123 Systems) is based in the USA. The car is assembled in the Valmet Automotive plant in Finland. As you see, it is a truly international project. However, it is questionable whether the holistic approach actually works.

Configuration-wise the Th!nk is either a two-seater with a big trunk, or

Th!nk is a rather good-looking car and, as one of the few electric cars to have successfully undergone a crash test, is apparently heading for a bright future.
(Photo by Knut Bry, Courtesy of Th!nk)

Th!nk's interior is befitting its Nordic image – extremely minimalist.
(Photo by Knut Bry, Courtesy Th!nk)

a 2+2 with no luggage compartment. The rear seatlets can be folded or unfolded to make space for kids or luggage. The Th!nk is one of two electric cars that has passed a crash test; the other being the Tesla Roadster. Th!nk weighs 1397kg, has a cleverly reinforced body, two frontal air bags, three-point seat belts, and ABS brakes. Although the car is small, it is relatively safe. The car is homologated (road-legal) in Europe, capable of highway driving, and should qualify for the majority of tax rebates and subsidies available. It will cost around £17-19,000 in the UK.

Electric cars make a great deal of sense in Scandinavian countries. For example, in Norway, amazingly, only 0.1 per cent of electricity is generated using coal plants. Electricity might not be cheap in Norway, but if a significant

number of people switched from internal combustion to electric cars, it would make a huge difference for Norway's environment.

The estimated range of 105 miles is calculated during summer with the heater off. Once on, though, the powerful heater (4kW) will shrink the range significantly. According to the manufacturer, the urban-only range might be as high as 126 miles (heater off) due to regenerative braking. The prices listed are non-inclusive of batteries, which means you'll get your battery pack on a lease; paying at least £60 per month.

Technical specifications

Motor power	30kW
Motor torque	90Nm (non-official)
Battery capacity	28.3kWh
Estimated range	105 miles
Max speed	65mph

Th!nk Ox

A five-seater from the Norwegian electric car gurus who already successfully produce the Th!nk City. Although the design resembles that of the smart forfour, it looks pretty good and will become a competitor for future family cars like the Nissan Leaf and others. The Ox will feature a solar panel on the roof to help power its greedy heating system and other on-board devices. The car promises to have a wireless web connection, an advanced navigation system, and a device that controls battery charge level and makes remote diagnostics and small maintenance or system reset possible. It is unclear when, and, if ever the car will become available on the market. Some sources suggest that the Ox is just an experimental model for the Norwegian company to explore the possible future of motoring; while there are other rumours that the car might be ready as early as 2012. The Ox will definitely offer a higher level of comfort than the current Th!nk model, but fans of Scandinavian technology should be patient for now.

Technical specifications

Motor power	100kW
Motor torque	n/a
Battery capacity	n/a
Estimated range	150 miles
Max speed	81mph

No, it is not a smart forfour; it's a concept of Th!nk's future family car – the Ox. (Courtesy Th!nk)

Toyota FT-EV

Toyota is one of the pioneers in the hybrid car field and it would be really weird if the company didn't have an electric car, or two, up its sleeves. Honestly, I'm puzzled as to why Toyota isn't at the forefront of electric car development. Well, apparently the company is even more electric-car-sceptical than Jeremy Clarkson! To get started on the journey, Toyota picked the funny little Toyota iQ and converted it into an electric car prototype following the Mini E approach, ie, removing the rear seats and filling the space with batteries. The car is codenamed FT-EV.

According to Toyota's American headquarters, little cars like iQ are where the company will focus its creativity. After the transformations that the hybrid Prius underwent, I was apprehensive that Toyota was more interested in proper-size cars. But since sales of the Prius (and hybrid cars generally) are falling in the USA, Toyota has obviously looked at expanding its green car strategy beyond the borders of hybrid technology. It's known that the car will be sold in the USA first in 2012; if everything goes to plan.

The cars are certainly oriented towards North America. The FT-EV made its debut at the 2009 Detroit Auto Show, and received some positive feedback. Although the work on the concept continues, and it's already unofficially announced to come to market in 2012, the constant lack of technical specification, and the fact that it's only a two-seater (not a match for the majority of other four-seat electric vehicles), may suggest that Toyota will end up offering a different electric car model in due course.

At the 2010 North American International Auto Show Toyota revealed a study in future motoring the FT-EV II. Unlike its more realistic predecessor, the II generation is a 2+2 seater with sliding doors, limited interior space, and resembles a small spaceship. At the same event the FT-CH compact hybrid

Toyota is not very keen on all-electric cars. This little runner, the FT-EV, could become the company's all-electric model. (Courtesy Toyota Motors)

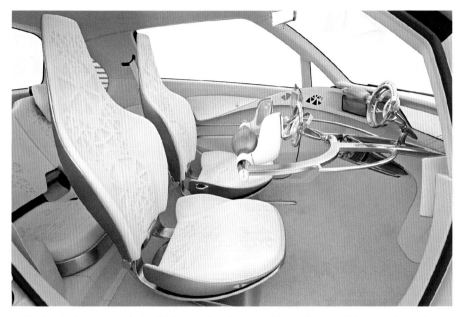

The interior is so futuristic that it's hard to imagine it would stay that way if the model went into production. (Courtesy Toyota Motors)

car prototype was revealed. You know what? I think Toyota doesn't really believe in the idea of all-electric vehicles. According to an official press release, Toyota's position is that, "Like hydrogen fuel cell vehicles, battery electrics will require the creation of infrastructure for recharging on the go. This issue of range is also a challenge to overcome. Even at 100 miles, BEVs as a primary mode of transportation do not yet offer what most consumers see as true mobility."

Toyota reminds us that all previous attempts at reviving the electric car have been a fiasco – Henney Kilowatt, EV1, and many others. In 1997 there was the Toyota RAV4 EV electric car that went on sale in California. The company managed to sell or lease 1484 cars, and the majority are still in running condition. However, the experience with previous electric car concepts has made Toyota more wary than other car makers. It claims that Toyota electric car programs were shortlived due to a lack of commitment from the market; the consumer's mindset wasn't ready to accept electric cars. However, the company does concede that the recent increase in environmental awareness (a little bit of brainwashing, a dash of 'greenwashing,' and a great deal of genuine concern for the environment), means that the market might be ready now. There will be a Toyota electric car in 2012. Let's see if it will be based on iQ, or if the company comes up with something else.

Technical specifications

Motor power	n/a
Motor torque	n/a
Battery capacity	n/a
Estimated range	50 miles
Max speed	n/a

Toyota Prius Plug-in

Toyota Prius is the first production hybrid car in the world and it is also the best selling one – well over one million units sold worldwide. However, the conventional Toyota Prius is of no interest to us. It's the next generation plug-in hybrid car that we're waiting for. A plug-in hybrid can be charged from an outlet just like an electric car, and it can cover short distances without ever starting the petrol engine. In Toyota's case the 'free' range is a maximum of 14 miles. After the electricity is used up or if the speed exceeds 60mph, a 98bhp petrol engine kicks in. The energy from regenerative braking is again deposited into the batteries.

The first test units have been built already, but it will be in the second half of 2011 when the cars will finally go on sale. Once available, the Prius Plug-in will be one of the most efficient petrol cars on the market, with an estimated 51mpg fuel consumption and 104g per mile CO_2 emissions.

Technical specifications

Motor power	98bhp / 60kW
Motor torque	142Nm / 207Nm
Battery capacity	5kWh
Estimated range	14 miles
Max speed	106mph

Twike

Twike, short for 'twin bike,' is a hybrid vehicle that combines electric propulsion with muscle propulsion. In essence it's a glorified velomobile, but it is so unusual that you simply cannot help but admire it. There is quite a bit of history behind the Twike. It made its debut at the 1986 World EXPO in Canada. Created by a group of Swiss students, it was only a velomobile (without the glorification bit). It re-emerged as a DC-motor powered hybrid in 1991. Soon, a company was established to run an experimental production batch of Twikes. Since then the name of the company and the ownership of the intellectual property have changed. The first time the Twike

Toyota in its element – the much-anticipated Prius Plug-in hybrid car. (Courtesy Toyota Motors)

Twike – yes, it's a velomobile, but a special one. (Courtesy Benjamin Zurbriggen from Swiss Twikeklub, shox.ch and twikeklub.ch)

gained recognition as a production vehicle was during the Mendrisio experiment in Switzerland (you can read more about it in chapter 8).

Twike can be registered as a motorbike, and it's unlikely you would have problems doing so anywhere in the world; velomobiles and motorbikes are legal almost everywhere. I won't say too much about safety ... Twike is certainly not for everyone, but if you feel comfortable riding a motorbike or cycling amongst busy traffic, you'll find that it offers a better level of safety than a conventional two-wheeled vehicle. Comparing it with a car ... well, I can't really because it's not a car.

Driving a Twike feels like using a computer game or simulator. It doesn't have a steering wheel – instead, there's a joystick in the middle of the cockpit.

Despite the production problems, Twike is one of the best-selling electric vehicles in the world. No-one really knows how many have been sold, but it's estimated to have reached between 800 and 1000 units worldwide. Although there is a lot of an uncertainty

concerning the manufacturing of the vehicle, it is still being made to order, and sold here and there. The real issue with the Twike is that there is no set vision or strategy, but I'm sure they'll get there, eventually. In the UK the base price for a Twike is £14,980 including VAT, batteries not included. The smallest Li-ion battery pack costs £4580, plus a mounting unit – £670. Thus, the total comes to £20,230. The base price in the USA is around $30,000, including batteries. It's quite expensive, but the sense of freedom riding a Twike must be amazing. Certainly, the price should come down if the Twike is to have any future.

The range and other specs of the vehicle depend on the battery pack you choose. For those who like pedalling, the minimum battery pack will be sufficient.

Technical specifications

Motor power	5kW
Motor torque	n/a
Battery capacity	various
Estimated range	25-150 miles
Max speed	52mph

Venturi Fetish

In normal circumstances I probably wouldn't bother with the Venturi Fetish, as it's a hyper-expensive, limited edition sports car. Only 25 will ever be made, and few will make it over the borders of Monaco. However, as there are several interesting concept cars brewing within Venturi's stables, I just cannot skip them.

Venturi Fetish is the world's first meant-for-production electric sports car. It made its debut in 2002 Geneva Motor Show (the first time anyone mentioned the Tesla Roadster was 2006). The Jamais Contente of 1899 by Camille Jenatzy doesn't count because it was intended to satisfy one man's passion for (or obsession with) speed. Unlike Venturi's concepts, the Fetish is nothing revolutionary. It's just a great quality sports car with a price tag of £250,000, but it's unlikely that you'll see one in Britain or the USA.

Technical specifications

Motor power	180kW
Motor torque	220Nm
Battery capacity	28kWh
Estimated range	155 miles
Max speed	100mph

Venturi Fetish – the first-ever electric sports car. It's a real beauty. Although it appeared before the Tesla Roadster, it has yet to make an impression on the electric car market.
(Photo by NiCO, courtesy of Venturi, venturi.fr)

Venturi Astrolab

One of the most unusual cars of the future is the Venturi Astrolab; a plug-in solar vehicle. Its top surface is covered in a 32 square foot (3.6m²) modern photovoltaic panel with a nano-prism film on top to make the most of the sunlight. The two-seater is so light that it can get by with a 16kW motor and still achieve a top speed of 75mph. The new owner of the troubled old French car manufacturer – Monaco-based Gildo Pallanca Pastor – compares the Astrolab with a sailboat: it's silent and uses nature's power for propulsion. The necessary safety level is achieved due to using an ultra light F1-like monocoque construction. The driver and passenger are both encased in a tough carbon-fibre cradle that is situated in the middle of a significant volume of energy absorbent material. I'm aware that this technology is not cheap, but it's getting cheaper gradually. It is not necessary to use all the expensive materials and technology of F1 – there are more affordable alternatives suited for mass production and currently overlooked by the big manufacturers. In the event of a roll-over, there are two safety hoops to prevent serious injuries.

The solar cell has a 600W output and it is estimated by Venturi that the energy generated during a single day would be sufficient to cover 12 miles without using batteries. This is actually a very conservative estimate. Watch out for the Astrolab; it's the beginning of a very exciting branch of vehicle development, and we'll certainly see this niche saturating quite quickly within the next decade or so.

When it comes to production (providing the company can find sufficient funding) the Astrolab will be classified as a heavy quad bike. It does ring alarm bells, but if the production model has the same monocoque

Venturi Astrolab making an appearance on a public road. It's a real head turner!
(Courtesy Venturi)

construction as the prototype, it would still be relatively safe.

Technical specifications

Motor power	16kW
Motor torque	50Nm
Battery capacity	7kWh
Estimated range	68+12 miles
Max speed	75mph

Venturi Eclectic

If it came out of the lab of a little known start-up we would probably laugh at the Eclectic, but as there's a certain credibility associated with Venturi, let's try not to. A car equipped with a wind generator? I mean, how far can some people go? This is what Eclectic stands for – it is built to generate the majority of its 'fuel' onboard. There are photovoltaic panels on the roof and if you catch the right sort of wind, you can deploy a small wind generator. Obviously, if you're moving, a hoisted propeller will increase the car's drag coefficient to a level where it's all getting silly, but when the car is stationary, there is nothing wrong with this concept. And if you park your Eclectic in an open space where there's plenty of daylight and some occasional bursts of wind, I don't see why you couldn't forget about the wall plug. You should be able to do some ten to 20 grid-free miles daily depending on how sunny your outlook is and how windy your parking space.

Although it looks like a robot, you must admit that it is quite a smart attempt, and the designer certainly knows a thing or two about shapes and proportions. The proposed price of the vehicle is in the region of EUR15,000 including the batteries.

What about safety? Honestly, I don't know. It depends on how confident Venturi is about its car, and whether the company will do some goodwill safety tests (goodwill because under the current regulation it won't be obliged to do so). The Eclectic is only four inches longer and eight inches wider than the REVA. Judging from the early press images, however, there will be more legroom for the driver and passengers because it's a three-seater. Also, the occupants' heads will be further from the sides. The Eclectic, being classified as a quad bike, will probably be less safe than a

Venturi Eclectic – the car that can generate its own electricity. Without the door ... the weather is okay today. (Courtesy Venturi)

conventional car, but it's hard to judge something that I haven't seen in the flesh.

Technical specifications

Motor power	4kW
Motor torque	52Nm
Battery capacity	7kWh
Estimated range	31+15 miles
Max speed	28mph

Venturi Eclectic with the door – for when the weather's not okay. (Courtesy Venturi)

eight
Electric car history

Most historians will agree that mass production of automobiles began with an electric car. Although the first commercial car was built by Karl Benz in 1888, it was only in 1900 that proper production factories were built in France and in the USA. The first stages of electric car history were more dynamic. In 1888, Moritz Immisch, an Anglo-German engineer, and Radcliff Ward both founded public transport companies in London. Moritz Immisch opted to make electrical trams and small cars, while Radcliff Ward produced electric omnibuses for the city. They soon went out of business, but across the ocean an electric revolution began.

During the last decade of the 19th century in the USA several small bicycle and engineering companies started producing three-wheeled electric vehicles, but the real breakthrough came in 1898 when, in Cleveland, the first mass-production electric vehicle

company – Baker Electric – was established. Who knows, if events had turned out differently, perhaps Cleveland instead of Detroit would have become the capital of the American motor industry? Before 1905, Baker Electric built around 800 cars per year – almost twice as many as Oldsmobile did petrol cars.

It all started rather early. In 1834, Thomas Davenport, an uneducated blacksmith from Vermont, USA, built a car with a small primitive electric engine. Although the idea of transforming electrical energy into mechanical was pioneered by Brits Michael Faraday and William Sturgeon, it was Davenport the blacksmith who first saw the potential and used an electric motor to power a wheeled device. After a few years, and independently from Davenport, Scotsman Robert Davidson became interested in electric propulsion and built an electric locomotive that was considered too expensive to run. Alas,

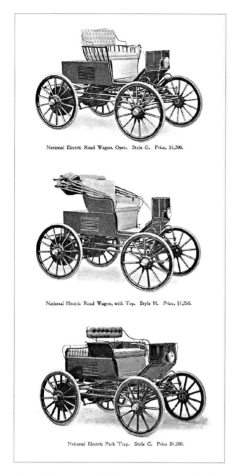

National Electric Road Wagon. Oper. Style G. Price, $1,200.

National Electric Road Wagon, with Top. Style H. Price, $1,250.

National Electric Park Trap. Style C. Price $1,200.

Early 20th century USA; a very popular electric car range by National Electric. (Courtesy Charles Test, chuckstoyland.com)

bad timing – steam locomotives were simple to produce and cheap to run. Another Scotsman Robert Anderson built a usable little electric cart. The biggest failing of both designs was the limitations of the recharging system. Rechargeable batteries weren't available in those days, so every time a battery became depleted, it had to be discarded and replaced by a new one. Another stage of development

in electric car history began in 1859 when French physicist Gaston Plante invented the lead-acid battery – the first rechargeable battery. Camille Alphonse Faure, another Frenchman and an acclaimed chemical engineer, significantly improved the design of the lead battery in 1881. Although the resources were there, until 1888 no-one ever dared to think about building electric cars for public use. Fred Kimball from Boston built an electric car that could do up to 15 miles between recharges. It was a noteworthy achievement, even if top speed was just 5mph. Initially it seemed possible that Kimball's design would go into mass production but, for some reason, it never happened.

Europe never warmed to the idea of electric vehicles. Although Gustav Trouve showed an electric tricycle at the 1881 Paris Exhibition, it was never taken seriously. In 1899 Camille Jenatzy made the sceptical Europe look at electric cars from a new perspective. He set the land speed record in his torpedo-like electric car called Jamais Contente (Never Satisfied). He certainly had to be satisfied in the end as he managed to squeeze 66mph out of his wheeled torpedo. Although Jenatzy was the superhero of Belgium, and an idol to many automobile enthusiasts across the Europe, the Old World decided not to embark on the manufacture of electric cars.

Meanwhile, in the USA, a real electric car boom had started. Before the end of 1910 there were at least 25 companies in the USA making electric cars. Having started with New York taxis – the world's first significant fleet of electric cars – the electrification spread to the private sector; and it seems ladies in particular were fond of electric cars as they didn't have a crank-starter nor tedious gear shifting.

One of the mightiest players of the

A lady driver – unheard of then – is depicted on this early 20th century Studebaker electric car ad. Women were reluctant to drive petrol cars because starting them was a challenge. (Courtesy Charles Test)

American electric car golden era was the Woods Motor Company. Its golden years were from 1899 to 1918. The fact that Woods began its activities with a ten million dollar start-up capital was evidence of how firm the belief was in the future of electric cars. It was an unbelievable sum of money for that time. The first electric vehicle was priced around $400, but, by the turn of the century prices had risen to $3000. Woods was an innovative company, but what it is most famous for is probably introducing the electric car to the Hawaiian islands. Until 1902 Hawaiians weren't aware of the existence of powered vehicles, and they received the first electric cars with reverence and admiration. In 1915 Woods started selling a hybrid car with both electric and petrol motors.

Detroit Electric is probably the most well-known name in electric car production. In the 20-year period between 1907 and 1927 it assembled over 12,000 passenger vehicles. Around 1912 it was selling almost 2000 cars a year. Although Detroit Electric models were quite heavy due to the battery packs, they could achieve a range of 80 miles on an advanced nickel-iron battery. So, you see, we haven't moved away significantly from what the early 20th century electric cars could achieve ... The range is pretty much the same, but speed and safety are improved.

Steam carriages were quite popular at the end of the 19th century but, because of the electric car, they never really took off. They were comparatively hard to use. It sometimes took more than 30 minutes of heating for the steam to form and the car to start.

Petrol vehicles showed promise, but because of the lack of an automatic starter they were unsuitable for women and physically weaker people. It also took a certain skill to operate a petrol car (who could possibly make sense of all those cranks, levers and knobs?), and petrol was hard to come by. Electric cars were much simpler. Some chemists sold petrol, but there were no petrol stations, whereas electricity was available to the majority of townsfolk – well certainly to those who could afford to spend $3000 on a car.

Most Americans believed that the electric car was the real solution to the growing transportation problem, which is why it came as a surprise to many to see electric cars disappearing from the streets as suddenly as they had appeared.

The person who delivered the first blow to electric cars (the oil lobby and a lazy consumer would soon finish it off) was Charles Kettering; the man who introduced the electric starter for petrol cars. As hand-cranks disappeared, motoring became more accessible to the general public.

The second blow was the sorry state of the road infrastructure of the USA. You might be wondering why the wheels of the first cars were so big. It certainly must have been hard for a gentleman wearing tight trousers or for a lady clad in a splendid long dress to clamber into the high vehicles. Although to some extent wheel diameter was dictated by the unsatisfactory gear ratios in the early gearboxes, the main reason for keeping them big was the condition of the roads.

We cannot put the whole blame on Mr Kettering, though. Early electric cars lacked power. That could be especially felt on the bad American roads. Even a modern car wouldn't go far in the Wild West countryside. The situation in towns wasn't much better. Although some of the streets were cobbled, the majority weren't; it was all gravel and dirt. An electric car was often useless in such conditions. Although frisky enough on a smooth surface, they were rubbish at off-roading. Early electric cars were heavy because they had to carry huge battery packs. For example, an average electric car concealed some 50-60 rechargeable batteries under its body, making some bigger models weigh as much as two tonnes. A petrol car was lighter, it didn't stick in the mud so badly, and it had relatively more power. Besides, electric cars were suitable only for townspeople – electrification of rural regions began in the 1930s thanks to President Roosevelt. Farmers had to drive something, and electric cars weren't suitable for them.

The lack of a unified voltage standard spelled the end for the electric car in terms of garnering a mass following. Seeing an outlet in the wall, you couldn't really be sure what flowed through it – alternating current or direct current and, what voltage? Furthermore, the grid was pretty unstable, and sometimes it was a challenge to recharge a car even if you lived in the posh part of town. The famous physicist Thomas Alva Edison promoted direct current (his company distributed direct current), whereas Westinghouse, the first American power supply giant, tried to persuade people to adopt alternating current because it was cheaper and more efficient. In the end Westinghouse won, but the electric car producers were confused – they couldn't build cars and charging devices that would suit everyone and all electricity supplies. All early electric cars used direct current, and eventually the manufacturers sold their cars kitted with a rectifier and a stabilizer – a big unwieldy device, and very expensive as well. It's funny that the standard equipment of an electric car included only the cable; the client had to buy the rectifier separately.

Petrol became more widely available and cheap, and as the petrol stations sprung up and all chemists stocked petrol, no-one really worried about fuel consumption. In 1915 an electric car still cost anywhere between $1500 to $2500 to buy ($2500 in 1910 is around $50,000 today). As petrol engine technology advanced, it was soon possible to buy a petrol car for as little as $500, and they were nearly three times cheaper to run than an electric vehicle.

Electricity was the prerogative of the rich, but everybody wanted to drive a car. Only the richest townspeople could afford to plug into the power grid. In 1905 one kWh of electricity cost 20-40 cents depending on the provider; and 40 cents was a lot of money. One litre of petrol was just short of a cent. And if we're talking distances, one litre of petrol can get you much further than

Henney Kilowatt – the first modern, transistor-based electric car. (Courtesy Feelgood Cars)

one kWh of electricity. Today it's quite a different story. People have learnt to produce electricity really cheaply (at a cost of polluting the environment) and it is now up to five times more economical to drive an electric car than a petrol car.

By the 1930s every electric car manufacturer had closed or changed its profile.

There have been attempts to reinvent the electric car over the years. In 1959, for example, Henney introduced the Kilowatt – a small car based on the Renault Dauphine – incorporating modern technology not very different from that used in electric cars today. By the mid-1950s, though, transistors were available, and these made things very simple and efficient; from both a driving and a production perspective. Transistors meant that a simple controller could be built that would make the batteries and power transmission more effective. Henney managed to attract quite a substantial amount of investors, but in the end the money raised wasn't enough to market the car to the sceptical and imperceptive public. Although around a thousand cars were produced, barely half of them were sold. The Henneys could reach speeds of 60mph and go more than 60 miles on one charge, despite their rather primitive lead batteries. Several of the Henney Kilowatt units are still running and are

95

A unique moment in history – Ford is testing an electric car prototype shortly before the first wave of electric car popularity came to an abrupt end.
(Courtesy Ford Motors via Creative Commons Licence)

even used as everyday family cars by enthusiasts.

During the 1960s and '70s several attempts were made to build a super-efficient electric car (it's usually in times of fuel crisis that people start thinking about alternatives).

Scottish Aviation spent a couple of years developing a fun two-seater called the Scamp 13A. However, the batteries were so inefficient that the car could barely cover 20 miles on a charge. Instead of sourcing a better set of batteries, the Scots decided to call it a day and move on with working on their bespoke Jetstream aircraft.

One of the rare commercial endeavours that actually sold a few cars was the Anglo-Greek Enfield project. Constructed in England and financed and built in Greece, the Enfield was a funny little car initially aimed at the hospitality industry. In the 1970s it was impossible to make an electric car road-

legal in Greece, hence the company's initial plans to build up an electric rental-car fleet for tourists coming to the country never materialized, and it ended up trying to persuade Brits to

Ford Comuta of 1967 – another attempt to create an efficient little car; just on the brink of the first major oil crisis. (Courtesy Ford Motors)

buy them; and some did. From 100 cars manufactured, a handful were sold. Now, they are a rarity, and, considering the revived interest in all things electric, should one come up for auction, it would fetch a tidy sum.

The resurrection of modern day electric cars started in the early 1990s when California Air Resources Board (CARB) passed a highly controversial law that required local car manufacturers to get their act together and start producing zero emission vehicles at once! American car giants had been playing with all sorts of different alternative motoring prototypes since the '60s, but none of the daring prototypes ever made it to the production line. Now things were about to change, and those who didn't obey would have been barred from selling cars in California – one of America's richest states. Car manufacturers and oil lobby groups kicked up a huge fuss, but California remained rock-solid about its new policy. As General Motors had just shown its new all-electric car prototype (the GM Impact), it decided to give it a go. All the rest followed along reluctantly, but only GM managed to produce a significant amount of electric cars before the controversial zero emission car bill was finally revoked.

The Impact prototype evolved into the EV1 production vehicle. Its retail price would have been nearly $40,000, but GM had no intention of selling it. The car was leased to pre-selected customers so that they could be called back should something go wrong. The monthly lease fee was in the region of $500, and there were few people around who fancied leasing a two-seater with an alien powertrain and a high monthly fee. However, actor Tom Hanks and another 800 people embraced the idea, but despite growing enthusiasm, the electric car project had

Scottish Aviation Scamp, 1970. (Courtesy DeFacto via Creative Commons Licence)

The Anglo-Greek Enfield Neorion was meant to entertain tourists. (Taken from an old Enfield Neorion advertisement)

pretty much reached its end. GM could have leased out more vehicles, or even sold the odd one, but it would have never been a profitable endeavour.

Apparently the leasees loved the EV1 because, when the project was officially cancelled in 2002, many wanted their lease extended, and even offered to self-maintain the car and promised not to claim any responsibility from GM. Nevertheless, all the cars were seized from the bewildered customers and destroyed.

Paralleling the EV1 was the Chevrolet S-10 EV electric pick-up. Almost 500 units were assembled between 1997 and 1999, but only 60 were ever sold, with the remaining fleet going to a scrapyard. It was probably the first production car to pioneer an on-board heat pump. Today, it's Audi which is actively promoting and developing this interesting idea.

From 1995 to 1999 GM's competitor Chrysler came up with its own electric car conversion. Based on the Dodge Caravan, the Chrysler TEVan was never intended for the general public. If it was sold, its retail price would have been $120,000 (which shows you how unfeasible it was to produce electric cars in the 1990s). Frankly speaking, the endeavour still hovers between feasibility and disaster, but at least today the manufacturers have a slight hope that after twenty years of strange political games and an obvious lack of interest from the consumer, we're finally ready to accept the electric car.

In 1996 the Solectria Corporation started testing a design similar to the EV1 (with the same streamlined body and hidden rear wheels). Unlike the EV1, though, the Sunrise was a four-seater, and, despite that, had a lower drag coefficient of 0.17 (the EV1 had 0.19, while the standard for a mass-produced street car is around 0.30). The Sunrise was as efficient as it's possible to be, and, allegedly, still holds a range record for a full-size electric car: it once did 375 miles on one charge, driving on public roads (as opposed to special testing facilities where the majority of other electric cars are tested). Nothing came of the Sunrise project, ultimately due to lack of interest form the public. There are attempts to revive the Sunrise in the form of a DIY kit-car, and this might still be successful; who knows? Being a very efficient car, it deserves a place in the market.

Eco enthusiasts didn't take the end of the GM EV1 project too well. They accused General Motors of sabotaging the EV1, and oil magnates of hard-lobbying and even bribing the officials to get the ruling scrapped. Although

Solectria Sunrise – the most unfortunate failure of the modern electric car era. The Sunrise was a magnificent car, and is currently being redesigned by Lee A Hart as a kit car.

their frustration is understandable, many experts believe that it was neither. It doesn't take too much reasoning to understand that if you're in business, you don't want to produce things that cause you terrible losses. From GM's perspective, cutting the oxygen on EV1 was simply damage limitation: having spent in excess of $1 billion (not counting the millions spent on the sporadic and ill-judged advertising campaign), GM managed to lease out just 800 electric cars. A smaller company would have simply collapsed after such a run of bad luck, but for a giant like GM, a billion here or there didn't make a huge difference, although, I bet it hurt both the pride and the budget.

Noticing that a zero emission vehicle revolution was brewing in America, several European automakers decided to show an electric car model to avoid being considered old-fashioned. Did any of them really think electric cars would go mass-market in the mid 1990s? I very much doubt so.

Between 1995 and 1998 Volkswagen produced an experimental batch of 200 Golf Citystrommer electric cars. A proper four-seater, it had a 22kW motor and a big pack of lead-acid batteries under the floor. It's most unusual feature was that the Citystrommer Golf, being an electric car, consumed diesel ... to power the heater. Using an electric heater was out of the question because the battery output was limited.

There were several other attempts to build an electric car in Europe. There was a Peugeot 106 Electric, Arton-Renault Twingo, and the Renault Elektro Clio. The latter proved that a 19kW (26bhp) engine is enough to get a four-seater around on its daily errands, but none of these was a commercial success.

General Motors EV-1. Don't look for a conspiracy theory here – it was an interesting experiment with no potential to make money for GM. (Courtesy GM)

By 1999, the whole worldwide effort to present a reliable and economically feasible electric car had fizzled out. Only small, rather 'geeky' start-ups and privately funded electric car ventures remained: the mid '90s did give us the REVA (India), Th!nk (Norway), Twike (Switzerland), and several others.

Even if there really was something fishy behind the demise of EV1, it's clear that the consumer wasn't ready for an electric car in the mid 1990s. There was almost no competition in the market, hence no choice, and the consumer doesn't like that. The cars would be too expensive for the average family to buy and maintain, the batteries were too heavy, and the range too short. The most important reason, however, was that there was no information available on electric cars. You cannot say to the consumer: "Please buy this thing because it's good for our planet! I cannot really explain what this thing is, but trust me, we'll all benefit!"

Although the last successful mass-produced electric car is widely regarded to have been made in the 1920s, electric cars, silent and invisible, have been around us constantly; milk floats, tow tractors, factory cars, delivery vehicles, and golf carts. For example, Bradshaw Electric, in the middle of Cambridgeshire has been making several hundreds of electric cars every year for 25 years without anyone really noticing. Many businesses are dependent on good quality electric cars, and the way they run their fleet hasn't really changed through the decades: charge overnight and drive during the day – just like we could potentially do with passenger electric vehicles. Besides, commercial electric vehicles don't cost over $100,000, so maybe those who say that producing electric cars is extremely expensive and unfeasible, are exaggerating?

We've been talking about electric cars again for more than 20 years and it is only now that people are beginning to grasp the whole idea, and are beginning to consider an electric car as something more-or-less serious and tangible. If you look back at even the most recent past, the public image of the electric car was never shiny enough to be considered a marketable and feasible object.

Real life testing
If you've been following the development of electric cars over the last few years, you'll be familiar with the news stories that go: "Company X has produced a number of testing vehicles and leased them out to hand-picked members of public to determine how the car fits with the modern lifestyle of an everyday motorist, and to find out if the model is feasible for production in the near future." Of course, "the near future" is always being delayed. Real life testing is one of the most reliable ways for a manufacturer to weed out a car's faults before it hits the production lines. There's nothing wrong with the testing, it's just disappointing when (as in the majority of cases) no results are published, and the models are just scrapped, renamed, or delayed. One of the first mass-scale electric car road test campaigns started in Switzerland in

1995 when there were very few electric cars available. It was dubbed the 'Lightweight Electric Vehicles Project' or the 'Electric Swiss Village.'

In 1994 the Federal Office of Energy chose Mendrisio town as the pilot municipality for the first large-scale electric car fleet test. Mendrisio is a beautiful, busy little town with 6500 inhabitants. Although the target of 350 electric cars in operation was never achieved, the FOE really succeeded in carrying out a fleet test. By mid-1999 almost 180 electric cars were sold in Mendrisio. It wouldn't have been possible without a substantial subsidy to entice people into buying an unknown car. The Federal Office of Energy offered a 60 per cent discount to anyone within the proximities of Mendrision who would agree to take part in this experiment. In four years the town's electric car fleet had covered a total of 680,000km (422,000 miles). The majority of the participants were private owners, but businesses were involved too, and everyone was generally quite happy with the new electric cars. The officials monitoring the pilot project came to the

The spectacular region of Mendrisio was a perfect place to start a large-scale, real-life, electric car testing programme. (Courtesy Patrik Tschudin via Creative Commons Licence)

Mitsubishi i MiEVs are being tested in Coventry and Birmingham under the guidance of CABLED. (Courtesy cabled.org.uk)

conclusion that an average four-wheel/four-seat electric car consumed around 24kWh per 100km (0.38kWh per mile). Just ten years on and that consumption figure has improved. Now, 0.25kWh per mile is standard for a decent-size electric car. The following four-seaters took part: Peugeot 106 Electric, Citroën Saxo, Renault Clio, Fiat Seicento Elettra, and Honda EV Plus. There are records that show that the Seicento Elettra was the most efficient of all – consuming just 0.23kWh per mile. It was also the first chance for the Twike velomobile hybrid to shine. Quite a few of those were sold in Mendrisio and, in a combined cycle (partly on pedal power, partly on an electric motor) it showed 0.15kWh per mile consumption.

Have you heard about the Mendrisio experiment before? It's quite possible that you may not have, since there were people who didn't want the good news about the Mendrisio fleet test to spread beyond the town's borders. People involved in certain industries felt extremely uneasy about publicizing the results of the experiment. From the marketability point of view the Mendrisio fleet test looks very promising. The fact that around 200 people within a busy community can enjoy driving electric cars provides hope that, by employing the right strategy, the electric car advance won't get killed for the third time.

However, being an engineer, I can see that many car manufacturers would be very wary about all this electric car hype. It will be years or even decades before producing electric cars will become a profitable endeavour for them. Many will continue developing green car technology just to keep in sync with their competitors, and it's possible that several of the independent electric car companies will go bust (as they've done before, all through the 1990s). The people brandishing the electric car flag are either enthusiastic journalists, environmentalists who cannot gather the courage to realize that electric cars do not provide zero emission,' or people directly or indirectly involved in supplies to the future electric car plants (those digging for lithium and those manufacturing the parts and equipment). There will be a lot of money made in this latest electric car wave, but it won't be made by the actual manufacturers of the electric cars. It is, however, a potentially nice niche in the long run; and if the experts are right, that by 2025 at least ten per cent of the new cars sold will be either hybrids or electric cars, the money will start rolling in.

You may argue that there would have been no positive results in Mendrisio without the whole project being subsidized, and you might be right. The price is still an issue with electric cars and, as you can see from the 'Electric cars and money' chapter, governments are ready to provide a subsidy for those who opt for so-called green cars. Unfortunately, they are rather reluctant to do anything to let those cars be green by failing to develop greener means of generating electricity.

nine

Electric car scepticism

For every environmental activist touting the electric car as the answer to world's motoring problems, there is one grumpy sceptic counting the cons of electric cars and telling you how ludicrous the whole idea is. If you look back in history, in spite of people generally being curious and inventive, all the big ideas are often met with a huge dose of initial scepticism. Internal combustion engined cars were no exception. When the first cars appeared late in the 19th century, people across Europe went on demonstrations, hoisting their slogans demanding that the noisy beasts be banned. Nobody will request banning electric cars, but I don't envy the guys working for marketing departments of electric car manufacturers; they face a tough challenge.

Scientists don't make the task any easier. In 2009 the National Academy of Sciences, USA carried out a study sponsored by the Department of Energy. The paper on the potential benefits of plug-in hybrid vehicles shed some light on some previously unknown aspects of green motoring. According to the scientists, even if the same course is maintained and the government keeps funding the development, there will be less than 40 million plug-in hybrid vehicles on the road by 2030. The more realistic figure is 13 million, which factors in the consumer scepticism and some other unpredictable issues.

Two hypothetical vehicles were used in order to simulate the model of future motoring. Vehicle-10 is similar to the Toyota Prius plug-in and can do ten miles without starting the petrol engine. Vehicle-40 is similar to the Chevy Volt, doing up to 40 miles on electricity.

It was found that Vehicle-10 would cost at least $3300 more to make than a conventional hybrid. 'Conventional' means a hybrid that cannot be plugged in and recharged. In operation, the Vehicle-10 would save its owner 20 per cent on the petrol necessary

A little bit of an apocalyptic fantasy. Will we ever
see this sort of protest demonstration?
(A cheeky remake of Marc Nozell's original
photo via Creative Commons Licence)

for older hybrids. If we stick to that
hypothetical figure of 40 million cars
by 2030, the full fleet of plug-in hybrids
would save the USA two per cent on
the current daily passenger car fuel
consumption. It would take hundreds
of billions dollars of taxpayers money
to maintain the current green car
development. That would turn out to
be a very costly two per cent savings,
with the positive impact not really worth
the fuss. The Vehicle-40 is likely to be
saving more than 55 per cent on usual
fuel consumption, but still, it's harder
to market because people do not
understand the philosophy behind the

car, and lack the confidence to jump
into an entirely new product.

The authors of this study have
estimated that plug-in hybrids would
be able to make a significant impact
only around 2050. Therefore, they are
suggesting a portfolio approach makes
the most sense – ie, not focusing on
a certain type of green car, but rather
spreading the effort over hydrogen,
electric cars, biofuel, and, what's more
important, making our current gas
guzzlers even more efficient.

The Academy found that the
biggest challenge of plug-in hybrid
vehicles would be the cost of
batteries and related equipment.
They have estimated that the cost of
manufacturing a Vehicle–40 can be as
much as $18,000 more than that for a
conventional passenger car of the same
size. The study also suggests that you'd
struggle to make any fuel savings during
the car's lifetime. This is not necessarily
true, however, as it largely depends
on your lifestyle: if you mostly do short
runs, you'll make savings; if you use
your hybrid just like any other petrol car,
you probably won't. Besides, when it
comes to cutting CO_2 – a hybrid takes
more CO_2 to manufacture and, while 50
per cent of electricity is being generated
in coal stations, the positive impact
of cutting emissions would be either
insignificant or none.

This comes as a shock to many of
us! At least the Department of Energy is
upfront and transparent, which shows
that common sense is still stronger than
corporative lobbying. Anyway, it was a
very surprising study and now many are
accusing the DoE of dual behaviour –
with one hand it gives grants and low
interest loans to electric car start-ups,
while with the other hand it's spoiling the
future marketing prospects by saying
that there's not much in the whole green
motoring thing.

A similar study was carried out in Denmark. The Danish Petroleum Industry Association has recently finished a study in collaboration with consultancy company Ea Energy Analysis. They compared the level of CO_2 emissions in different cars – petrol, diesel, electric cars, and hybrids – to find out which one is the best for the environment.

Surprisingly, when it comes to CO_2 emissions, there's not much to separate electric cars and diesels. According to the Danish study, CO_2 emissions from hybrids and electric cars are similar, while diesel cars emit only eight per cent more CO_2. Emissions from petrol cars are around 35 per cent higher compared with electric cars. Unfortunately, this study focuses on CO_2 and forgets about different kinds of pollution and eco-disruption.

The main problem is that, globally, the majority of electricity is generated in coal plants. Electric cars will begin making a difference when we switch to greener electricity. According to the study, around five per cent of the world's electricity will be renewable by 2015. It could rise to 15 per cent by 2025 – and that's when we will really begin seeing the benefits of driving an e-car.

This is quite a pessimistic (yet realistic) approach to the matter. However, please remember that if you switch to green energy today (for example, by installing photovoltaic panels on your roof), your green motoring starts today also.

The whole approach of how we use energy has to change for electric cars to make any difference. Sometimes I get the feeling that history might repeat itself, and this new electric car wave could last 20-odd years courtesy of a new, better and cleaner technology destined to replace it. Electric cars weren't too practical in early 20th century America, and, despite improved technology, don't seem like an ideal solution this time around. They are a *part* of the solution, but won't work for the environment on their own.

Ironically, we've chosen one of the scarcest elements on earth as a component of electric cars. As we discovered earlier, there's only enough lithium to produce 890 million battery packs. On the other hand, there is plenty of petrol. The US Department of Energy has now stopped estimating the amount of oil reserves in order to avoid further embarrassment. It has just said that there's definitely enough oil to sustain the world's energy demands until at least 2035. Russian scientists have claimed there's evidence that oil mysteriously reappears in empty oil wells. I'm not sure how credible that claim is, but the fact is we have some 20-30 years in which to establish additional alternative propulsion systems, sort out the hydrogen cars, and demolish the coal power plants to make electricity cleaner.

ten

Pros and cons of electric cars

Let's try to sum up the main pros and cons of electric cars to help you decide if an EV is for you. Because so far I may have sounded like an electric car sceptic (which I'm not), I'll start with the cons.

Cons
• **Zero emission hype:** Many eco-warriors (when you see a person chained to a tree, you know you've spotted one) want you to believe that an electric car is a zero emission vehicle; it is not. Your electric car is as green as the electricity that powers it. If your energy provider operates a thermo-plant (coal, oil) or buys electricity from abroad, your electric car may emit more grams of CO_2 per mile than a mid-size 4wd. If it is a hydro-station that provides the energy, alas, you are again nowhere near your environmentalist ideals. Hydro-stations totally upset the subtle eco-system of a river. I bet if you let the fish choose, they would rather you

Rather irrelevant, in fact. An electric car won't make too much noise.

drove a gas-guzzler than kill their spawn by installing another dam. I'm serious about this – large hydro-electric stations should be abolished. Read through the pros section for more info.

• **Infrastructure:** Somebody will have to pay for installing plug-in points and specialized service centres. Ever wondered who will pay for that? You will – with increased electricity bills and higher taxes.

• **Politics:** Electric cars are sometimes promoted because it's good 'business.' Many governments across the world want praise for creating new jobs and following the environmental guidelines. Who cares that it takes tens of thousands of pounds of taxpayers' money to create each job in the electric car industry? Who cares that it easily equals the carbon emissions of a full car fleet of countries like Albania to build and operate a full-scale electric car factory?

• **Expensive:** A single-seater Tango – $108,000, two-seater Tesla Roadster – $109,000, Twike – a mere velomobile – $30,000. If the price of electric cars doesn't fall big time, they risk being nothing more than rich-men's toys.

• **Many look weird:** Why? Why do the designers of electric cars think that in order to make a green car, it has to look like a design student's diploma project disaster? Have you developed a high-tech electrical powertrain? Well, mount it inside a proper car and you stand a much better chance of selling it. Is the squashed melon style the new trend to follow? I hope not. Luckily, there is some sanity left in the world of green motoring, and a considerable number of electric cars (largely those developed by the big companies) look pretty decent.

• **Low range:** Most electric cars can go for no more than 100 miles on a single charge. Using the currently available battery technology, and without an effective on-board electricity generation option, it is unlikely we can raise the range to more than 150 miles. Given this, the electric car will remain what it is now: an urban phenomenon. Do I need a car that cannot get me from the UK's South Coast to Scotland without a recharge? As much as I like the idea

of an electric car – I don't. But that's my personal opinion. I would probably sing another tune if I lived in a large city or if I was happy to use public transport for long-distance travel.

• **Silence:** An electric car might suffer from the Rolls-Royce effect (they're so quiet you cannot hear one approaching ... in fact, you can because the owner of the Rolls has put a Michael Ball CD on). It is not such a good thing being silent on the road, especially from the perspective of pedestrians. The electric car makers are considering ways of making EVs noisier. A rattle fitted to a wheel? Have you been to a superstore lately? Check one of their escalators, there will be this unbelievably annoying robot-woman's voice screeching: "You are now approaching the end of the run-way." That's 'health and safety' for you. We can use a similar system on an electric car. A built in system would broadcast: "A responsible driver is approaching in the latest-generation, zero emission urban vehicle."

• **Substance safety:** You are carrying a potentially hazardous substance under the floor. If the battery casing becomes ruptured, electrolyte could enter the interior. It's not sulphuric acid, but still, if not washed away immediately, it could cause permanent skin damage and/or health issues, depending on the electrolyte used.

• **Limited source of lithium:** The key material for the modern lithium-ion battery is, obviously, lithium. Extracting lithium is difficult, expensive, and it is a carbon-intensive procedure. When it's gone, it's gone. There are very few places in the world where lithium mines can be established, and these places can provide us with the valuable resource for only a limited time. Geologists have estimated that lithium is very scarce. The mines that are economically accessible contain no more than 15 million tonnes of the stuff. If we assume that in order to produce a battery with 1kWh capacity, 0.3kg lithium is needed. To make a battery set for the Tesla Roadster, we would need 16.8kg. It's quite easy to calculate that the earth can give us enough lithium to produce 893 million battery sets. If we've ever dreamt about launching electric cars on a mass scale, the lack of lithium might spoil the plans. It's known that the oceans contain unbelievable amounts of lithium (hundreds of billions of tons), but then the ocean contains gold as well; and have you ever seen a man trying to extract gold from the saltwater? On a positive note, it is possible to create a new generation of lithium-free batteries.

• **DIY:** Forget it. No more amateur mechanic delights. You cannot do any maintenance on your electric car unless your surname is Tesla.

• **Driveability:** Some electric cars are slow to accelerate. However, this is more of an issue for traffic-light racers, and it is an issue that is technically solvable. So, not really a con.

• **End of life:** When it comes to battery life, different sources give different figures. None can be taken too seriously because no electric car has been produced consistently enough yet. The estimate is anything between 40,000 and 200,000 miles. Both apex figures are very unlikely. 80,000 is probable, which means that an electric car's life is some seven to eight years. After that you just chuck it because the value of the vehicle will be much lower than that of a brand-new battery pack. But wait, can you just chuck an old electric

car away, or get rid of it through a scrappage scheme? No, you cannot. Somebody will have to pay to recycle and/or store the hazardous parts – this somebody will be you, and you'll pay for recycling either via added price or increased taxes. An idea: used Li-ion batteries can be sold on to wind turbine operators and even households using photovoltaics or wind generators. Although it is a good idea (you can store excess electricity in a battery), once the batteries are out of car manufacturers' hands, there's no control over how the new owners dispose of them.

• **Passive safety:** Regardless of what the manufacturers say, small cars are more vulnerable than big ones. Electric cars are often designed with a light structure to reduce weight, allow space for batteries, and increase the range. This approach can compromise safety. A car should have a crunch zone (something that absorbs crash energy), so basically it's a choice between 'crunch zone' and 'crunch bone.' Don't be fooled by the fairy-tale that the car makers sell small cars in order to provide you with more convenient parking options for your 21st century urban lifestyle. Small and simple cars are cheaper to make, and they often provide the maker with a better profit margin. Please check the Electric cars & safety chapter for more insights.

• **Blackouts:** Although we keep introducing new ways to save energy, the fact is that there is potentially not enough electricity to power our homes and businesses. Add electric cars to the grid and you get ... blackouts. Are there any candles left at your local newsagent? I suggest you buy some. Oops, I really didn't want to paint such a bleak picture, especially as I support the human quest for a green motoring source. So, let's look at the positive side now.

Pros

• **Money:** In the current situation it is five times cheaper to operate an electric car compared to conventional cars. This might soon change for the worse, but the price of electricity will never reach that of oil. Even if you can save two thirds off your motoring bill, it's still a very strong argument in favour of an electric car.

• **Fuel economy:** Driving a petrol car around a town means wasting energy at every traffic light or congestion spot. You don't cut off the engine every time you're caught out by red light, do you? That would certainly kill the starter in short order and make everyone else aggravated beyond sanity. So, the engine will run on idle and still consume fuel. According to the US Electric Auto Association, in Los Angeles alone 72 million gallons of fuel is wasted sitting in jams and waiting at the traffic lights. An electric car has none of that. Its motor will stop rotating if you take your foot off the 'throttle.' The electric car will consume power only when it moves (well, unless the heating or other auxiliary system is on).

• **Preservation:** By driving an electric car you help preserve the natural stock of fossil fuel. (If more and more motorists switch to electricity, we will even have the fuel to power our antique cars and drive them to our favourite shows, 100 years from now!)

• **Cheaper maintenance:** An electric car has fewer components, and electric motors are less prone to breakages (compared to internal combustion engines). It's cheaper to repair and you'll spend less money on lubrication.

• **Safety:** No more fires. You don't have to be afraid of being electrocuted, either. You will have fuses and circuit breakers taking care of safety. No really, have you ever heard of somebody being killed by a trolley-bus? For those not knowing what that is: a trolley-bus is a result of romance between a tram and a bus. It's been around since the 1950s, and is extremely popular in ex-Soviet countries. So, yeah, it is not possible to be killed by a trolley-bus unless you climb on its roof and stick your finger in a transformer or get run over.

• **Safety:** If constructed properly, an electric car is better at absorbing kinetic energy in an event of a crash. The batteries contain liquid which will absorb part of the impact. However, if you're driving a super-mini single-seater and have a high-speed crash, don't expect the EV to spare your life. Some argue that it is very unlikely thay you'll be involved in a high-speed collision driving a NEV, and, of course, it's no riskier than motorcycling, and thousands do that safely every day.

• **Handling:** some say that driving an electric car feels strange. Swap your limo for a mini (or vice versa) and that'll feel strange, too. Electric cars are certainly different, but, from many aspects – better. Batteries are usually installed under the floorpan, right between the axles. That gives the car a low centre of gravity and improves roadholding at high speeds and in sharp bends.

• **History:** Manufacturing and selling the electric car proved to be a viable business model in pre-Detroit America. Before the Big Three emerged, there were dozens of companies in the USA making or selling electric cars. One of the most prolific of them – Detroit Electric – managed to sell up to 2000 electric cars a year during its golden era (between 1910 and 1920). Despite the fact that those cars had a maximum range of only 40 miles, people were eager to buy. Why am I mentioning this? It gives you extra confidence if you can look back and derive lessons from a business that was once successful.

• **Precedent:** Electric cars are already being produced in huge numbers, in China, India and Japan. There is no accurate figure for this, though.

• **Somewhat greener energy:** If you can track down the energy source of your provider and you learn that the majority of it comes from nuclear power or wind, you can actually reduce your carbon footprint by a large amount by switching from petrol/gasoline to electricity. As many providers use a mixed source, or even buy electricity from abroad, you can never be sure.

• **Long-term economy:** As I mentioned before, the mass production of electric cars would shoot electricity prices through the roof. From the social perspective, higher energy bills would mean more responsibility in everyday use. It's been estimated that an average British family could save 30 per cent off its electricity bill by switching the lights off, boiling only the amount of water it needs, etc. However, higher electricity prices would make local councils take care of the street lights that are being left on during daylight hours.

Pros and cons of electric cars: conclusions

It is still your decision. Having said all those nasty things about electric cars, and having sung praises to them as well, I would still probably buy one as a second car if I had a large family or lived in a large city. Whether you need an electric car is really up to you. If you live in a large city and you are a frequent driver, you will actually save lots of money (on fuel, maintenance, parking, and, maybe, congestion charges) even despite the high initial buying cost. Theoretically, you will also keep your city cleaner by not emitting CO_2, however, your CO_2 will still be emitted somewhere else – by the company that generates electricity for your car. So, don't go there if your only goal is to save the blue whale from extinction. This large mammal doesn't give a fig whether your CO_2 'contribution' comes out of your car's exhaust or the power-plant's chimney.

My worry is that although many companies embark on electric car research/manufacture driven by genuine reasons, there are companies that try to overpromote electric cars purely for reasons of greed. So, be careful, but approach the new ideas with an open mind. It's a very exciting time and we cannot bury our heads in the sand and go on driving internal combustion cars forever. Things have to change and the electric car is one of the many possible directions towards that change.

Choosing an electric car now means investing in the future. Although at this very moment environmentally-wise it doesn't make much difference, if we do all turn our backs on this idea the big car companies will shut down their research labs and that will be a bad thing. Buying an electric car today means giving the industry much needed encouragement to continue developing all green motoring options. Do you remember I mentioned the portfolio approach to transportation? This means developing other alternative technologies, like hydrogen cars and air cars. Electric cars alone are not the answer to environmental problems, though they may well be a fundamental step foward.

eleven

Green home and green car

There is a concept that would potentially solve the problem of indirect emissions produced by electric cars. How would you like an electric car that freed you from the grid? It may sound like science fiction, but the first prototype of such a car was built in 1982 by Australian Hans Tholstrup. Yes, I'm talking solar vehicles here, and it isn't a joke.

Well, maybe I've gone too far by promising to get you off the grid. Although modern technology has come a long way, a solar cell that could power a four-seater car would be as big as the 'wings' on the Soyuz spaceship. Still, when you look at an average car, there are plenty of flat surfaces that are now simply wasted ... Look at the roof and the bonnet/hood, for example. An average family car has a suitable surface of 2.8 square metres (30ft²). If we clad it with flexible solar cells (more on that later) we would increase the range of an electric car by up to 20 miles! There's nothing that would be technically too

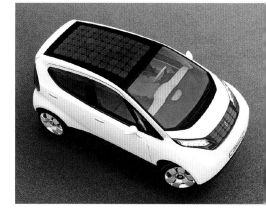

The photovoltaic panels on the roof can provide enough energy to power the ancillary equipment, and even put some juice in the batteries. (Courtesy Bluecar)

challenging or too expensive to produce. This is a relatively simple concept that will be employed sooner or later. Some manufacturers will start moaning about efficiency, feasibility, accountability, and

London Taxi with a roof finished in good old British Everflex. Many people are worried that having 'stuff' on car roofs will make them look ugly. Actually, from the designer's point of view, different textures can work well together. (Courtesy Norbert Schnitzler via Creative Commons Licence)

Generating electricity consumes huge amounts of clean water. Solar electricity will consume hardly any. (Courtesy Ed Yourdon via Creative Commons Licence)

other 'bilities,' while others will embrace this idea and pull it through to mass-scale production. There are at least three working prototypes that employ roof solar panels, and even Tesla is carrying out research in this field.

A solar car would still require batteries or a diesel-electric generator, but it would account for much less in the way of pollutants when compared to a hybrid or even a pure electric car.

Designers might protest that solar panels on the roof would spoil the visual appeal of a car. However, the truth is that the majority of cars in use are pretty much standard. Take a few middle-of-the range European or Korean cars, swap the badges and you'll manage to confuse anyone who doesn't watch *Top Gear*. No disrespect is meant, there are beautiful cars around, but it's unlikely that a bi-color scheme would spoil the overall impression. Look at the old London Taxi in the accompanying picture. Its black roof might as well be studded with solar cells; nobody would notice. It's actually possible that a solar car would look more elegant and techy than its colour-roofed cousin.

There's a long-lasting debate about

the manufacturing process of solar cells and how it affects the environment. Funnily enough, many 'tree huggers' have turned against photovoltaics, claiming that too much grey energy goes into producing them, and that during their lifetime they barely give back what they've consumed in manufacture. Well, true, due to the relatively low output of solar cells it really takes time to recoup the energy and money it takes to produce them; but things are getting better. With technology improving and with production output increasing (large-scale production is cheaper) it is very much a good idea to let the solar cell into our daily life.

The easiest way to evaluate all the pros and cons of solar cells is again to compare them with other means of producing electricity. Life cycle assessment is used by some environmentalists to measure the environmental impact of a service (supplying energy in this case) caused by its existence. There is no straightforward methodology in existence to evaluate the life cycle accurately. According to the Energy Research Centre of the Netherlands, each kWh generated by a solar cell is responsible for 25 grams of CO_2. It means that during the process of sourcing the materials and producing the cell, 25 grams of CO_2 have been emitted. It's really not that much. In the future, thanks to a better technology and mass-production, the life cycle emissions can go down to 15 grams of CO_2 per kWh. Currently, an average lifespan of a solar panel is 20-30 years. However, there are solar panels installed in the early 1960s that are still working. It means that by increasing the lifespan of solar cells, the life cycle impact will go down even further; ten grams of CO_2 per kWh is not impossible.

According to the same Dutch study, wind energy is the least carbon intensive at the moment. It's life cycle contribution is only 11g/kWh. The study reveals that a run of the mill photovoltaic panel based on silicon produced after 2006 can potentially pay back the input energy in just three years. More modern, thin-film systems can do the same in just 1.5 years. Besides this is a four-year old study, and the efficiency of solar cell manufacturing has improved. For the lifetime of a solar cell estimated to be more than 30 years, just 1.5 years to pay back the production energy is a very short period of time.

In comparison, a coal plant will have up to 1000 grams CO_2 per kWh. So, if cutting so-called greenhouse gasses is your priority, a 98.5 per cent cut is not bad at all! Natural gas has a life cycle impact of 500g/kWh, and the nuclear power as little as 50g/kWh, but my guess is that this calculation doesn't factor in the energy consumed and greenhouse gasses generated to safely store and maintain nuclear waste.

There are also other important factors that are not covered by the life cycle assessment, and which are often overlooked by solar cell opponents. How often do you consider the amount of clean water consumed by the thermo-electric plants? Water is necessary

to support the thermodynamic cycle of the power plant. In coal power plants it is also used to treat the fuel. According to Paul Gipe's *Wind Energy Comes of Age*, 1995, oil and coal power plants consume 1.6 and 1.9 litres per generated kWh respectively. The University of Strathclyde has estimated that an average UK household consumes 5000kWh of electricity annually. So, each year to power your house, up to 8000 litres of clean water are wasted. A human needs less than two litres a day to sustain life. Meanwhile, people around the world are drinking contaminated water or struggling to find any at all. In an ideal world, if no fossil fuel generated electricity were consumed, each UK household could supply 22 thirsty people with their yearly water measure.

Tiny amounts of water are consumed to produce photovoltaic cells and components for wind turbines. According to the aforementioned source, wind power accounts for 0.004 litres of water, and solar power 0.11 litres per kWh.

How much power can solar cells give me?

After we've learnt about all the nasty things that come out of fossil fuel plants, and especially coal plants, you might ask: what now? There's an interesting concept that many of us can try implementing right now, without waiting for the green future to come. It's the so called 'green-home-green-car principle'; where you go off the grid by switching to sustainable electricity (at least partly). You must have realized reading this far that if we don't change the way we generate and consume electricity, the whole electric car and hybrid car idea will bring little, or no, benefit whatsoever.

Taking some very rough and generalized estimates, a $1m^2$/$10.8ft^2$

A typical experimental solar car. It will take some time for one of these to appear on public roads. (Courtesy Steven Rainwater via Creative Commons Licence)

modern solar panel (identical to Nanosolar's thin film panel) will produce 0.1kW of power. How much energy it generates will be determined by where in the world you set it up. In Mid-Europe (southern England, northern France, eastern Europe) the level of solar irradiance is capable of generating significant amount of electricity for only around five hours a day. Multiplying 365 days in the year by five hours we get 1825 hours of efficient work. The remainder of daylight hours will be spent by the solar cell fooling around and putting meagre current through the wire. To reach the 5000kWh national average for family homes, let's divide it by 1825. The result – roughly 3kW is the system power you need. Obviously, if you consume less than 5000kW (some efficient households pull through with just 2000-3000kWh) adjust the formula to work out the necessary power. 3kW means you need a 30m²/323ft² rooftop panel and to pray for sunny weather. A fair amount of cloud will decrease the energy output, but you'll still get something out of the cells on those grey days. Don't believe me? Take your solar

powered pocket calculator and hoist it against the grey skies. It will work!

To support your electric car, you need half the energy necessary for an average family home. If we assume that the average electric car will consume 0.25kWh per mile and drive 10,000 miles per year, it works out at 2500kWh.

The cost of installing the panels is still relatively high, although First Solar – a company pioneering thin film photovoltaic systems in USA – claims it can produce panels at $980 per 1000W. The reality (at the time of writing) is a little different. On eBay you will still end up paying a minimum of £2 per watt (if you're lucky). So, your 30m² rooftop panel will come to £6000 (less if you don't consume 5000kWh a year). Yes, I know, I know, recession, depression, inflation, and all that, but let me put it this way: if you buy a good quality solar panel and install it yourself, it will go without much maintenance for at least 30 years. Once you've spent £6000, that's it. Now, divide £6000 by 30 years – it is a yearly electricity bill of £200, or £0.04 per kWh. Currently, the average retail price for a kWh of electricity is £0.10 ($0.165) in the UK and £0.07 ($0.12) in USA. But then solar panels are cheaper in the USA, so the savings are pretty similar – 50-60 per cent from what you're usually paying.

A recent development is solar roof tiles (why didn't I think of that?). They are so simple yet so clever. They are a little less efficient and a bit more expensive than thin film panels, but they look much better, and blend with the roof surface so that you barely see them.

Photovoltaics are very sensitive to a number of different factors. For example, they work to the maximum only when sunlight falls on them in a direct angle. Once the angle changes, the efficiency falls. Solar energy is not a solution for everyone. It only makes

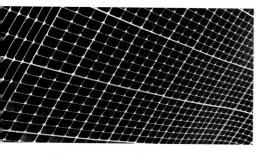

Put these on your roof and earn money. Feed-in tariffs have finally arrived in the UK. (Courtesy Steven Rainwater via Creative Commons Licence)

sense if you install the panels on a roof slope that is more-or-less south-facing, and not obstructed by trees or overshadowed by higher buildings.

A private wind generator might be used as a complimentary system. A self-installed domestic wind generator can produce anywhere between 400 to 1000kWh per year, depending on blade length and wind speeds. Low-speed generators with a special blade profile can pick up wind speeds of as low as 3.5m/s, which is great for suburbs. A DIY wind generator will rarely cost you more than a thousand pounds.

While browsing our electric car catalogue, you'll see that many car manufacturers are planning to mount solar cells on the roofs of their cars. Considering that the car constantly moves, and there are many objects that would do their best to cast a shadow on the rooftop solar cell, you cannot rely on solar energy to get you around. What solar cells can do, though, is help power headlamps and air-conditioning, and occasionally top up the battery with some free energy.

Feed-in tariff

A feed-in tariff is an amazing environmental policy that lets homeowners earn tax-free money on every kWh of green energy they generate using photovoltaics or wind turbines. If you produce more green energy than you can consume, there are three ways of dealing with it: buy more gadgets so that you consume more; sell some electricity to your neighbour; get the energy provider to buy some from you. Okay, I'm kidding; the first two were bogus. However, although the third option doesn't seem any more credible, it actually is. By installing a little device that connects your solar battery system to the national grid, you can feed all the excess electricity back into the grid and get paid for it. So you've changed roles with the energy supplier. You don't pay it any more, it pays you! Isn't that a lovely idea after all those years of energy dependency?

In the UK, the feed-in tariff was introduced on 1st April 2010. We have joined those 60-plus countries in the world that subsidize in-house production of green electricity. Currently, as much as £0.41 is being paid for each green kWh generated and consumed. It makes sense to start early because homeowners joining after 2013 might find themselves on a lower tariff. An extra £0.03 will be added per kWh sold back to the grid (ie: excess energy produced). These tariffs will apply to retro-installed photovoltaics. Newly-built houses with a planned rooftop solar panel will receive less. DIY is not permitted in the UK in order to qualify for the feed-in tariffs. The installation will have to be carried out by a technician certified by the Microgeneration Certification Scheme. Check with the Energy Saving Trust for more info.

Although a similar policy was adopted in the USA in 1978, it's actually Germany that has been at the forefront of this approach. It introduced feed-in tariffs in 1991, and the solar panel industry there is really booming.

In Germany, the current feed-in tariff is EUR0.57 per kWh. The feed-in contracts are generally signed on 20- or 25-year terms, but that should be more than enough to recoup the cost of your current solar installation and put some money aside for a future replacement or upgrade. You can make as much as £1500 tax-free per year (not counting the savings you make on your electricity bill) if you install solar panels or/and wind generator. Obviously the energy suppliers hate feed-in tariffs, hence there's a lot of negative press surrounding the issue.

BMW sees the feed-in option as a sure-fire way to make the energy consumed by electric cars a little bit greener. Prior to launching its Mini E tests in Australia (if the tests ever go ahead) the company has been asked by local journalists how it's going to persuade Australians to buy electric cars. As you remember from our little naughty coal table, Australia is one of the worst countries in the world when it comes to producing green electricity. Despite having tons more sunlight than we, and despite being one of the less densely populated countries, neither solar nor wind energy seems to be on the agenda, and it just keeps burning the 'Midnight Coal.' However, feed-in tariffs have been introduced in Australia, and one can see a certain positive shift towards greener energy there.

More future technologies
Do you remember I said that an electric car's working life is some seven years? A solar concept could increase it if the engineers get smarter. One idea is to 'structurize' the battery packs into several levels; for example, a fast access battery pack, a middle access pack, and a long range pack. During driving, all the energy generated by the solar cells goes directly to the engine.

When the vehicle is at a halt, the energy produced fills the fast access pack, and then the middle one.

When there's not enough sunlight the car will first access the 'fast' battery, and then move onto the middle one. So, if you're covering only short distances, or using the car in the city, the long range battery pack will rarely be used. This means fewer recharge cycles and a longer battery life. The fast access pack (the smallest one) will wear out more quickly, of course, but, as it's located separately from the other batteries, it can be easily replaced for a few hundred quid (replacing a whole battery pack as it is now would cost up to £5000). I think engineers will soon grab this idea and run with it.

Another concept to look out for is a full-wheel-drive electric car. I'm confident they'll start building those pretty soon. This idea is more than 100 years old – first conceived by the whiz-kid Ferdinand Porsche for Lohner. He built a car called Toujours Contente that had an electric motor inside each wheel hub. When Porsche did it, his motivation was to gain more space onboard by bringing the electric motors outside of the body of the vehicle. Quite unknowingly, he left us a hint that could transform the future of full-wheel-drive cars. For the modern concept, each wheel being driven by a separate motor means variable torque between axles, and even among the wheels, without a heavy and sophisticated transmission and differentials. All it needs is a tiny microchip that would detect if the wheel is stuck or spinning freely and vary the output it gets. It means that an electric SUV is not such a crazy idea after all. Transmission is possibly the most expensive and problematic part of a 4x4. Using Porsche's revolutionary layout, the car could easily do without one.

In electric cars, where everyone is

trying to save more space for batteries and passengers, getting the motor outboard would be a great opportunity. But as it is with all great opportunities, along comes a disadvantage. In the electric four-wheel drive case the disadvantage is the so called unsprung mass. By unsprung mass the car engineers understand the total mass of the components that are not carried by the vehicle's suspension. It includes the wheels, the suspension itself, axles, tyres, brakes, and other elements. Engineers have been trying to reduce unsprung mass in their designs for decades, especially on the racing track, and now I'm talking about piling on the pounds and rendering all their hard work useless. Mad, isn't it? Excess unsprung mass might worsen the road-holding, slow down acceleration, and increase the braking distance. But there are several clever ways around the problem.

Swiss-based non-conformist car designer Franco Sbarro has been playing with unconventional wheels since the mid 1980s. His most famous crazy-wheel car is the 1989 Sbarro Osmos concept car that featured a hubless wheel. Initially, the idea was intended merely to wow the public. Eventually, though, Sbarro came up with the idea that the entire propulsion system would be housed inside the wheel. Design students from Japan took this idea further and developed a bicycle without the usual chain mechanism. The bike would be powered by magnetic induction. You'd have to pedal in order to create a magnetic field that would then be transferred to the hubless wheel and make it rotate. Makota Makita and Hiroshi Tsuzaki from Tokyo were inspired by a Japanese high-speed, wheel-less train that employs magnetic superconductivity for propulsion. However, whereas the passengers of such a train can be protected from the

A hub motor is commonplace on electric bikes and smaller electric vehicles; however, potentially it can power future 4x4s. (Courtesy Alleweder)

Franco Sbarro's car of the future. He thinks that hubless wheels are a good idea. (Courtesy Espera Sbarro, e-sbarro.fr)

strong magnetic field by a special floor, the passengers of a car or a bike cannot.

However, it is possible to turn a hubless wheel into an electric motor. The outer rim being a rotor and the inside rim, a stator.

Anyway, in small cars the unsprung mass is not a very big problem. The motors inside the wheels would be relatively small, and they would also take over the brake function, thus making the conventional brakes unnecessary. Driving at speeds allowed within a city, the unsprung mass wouldn't alter the experience. Besides, there are many ways to reduce the unsprung mass. For example, it's possible to construct a wheel disc with spokes that work as springs.

twelve
The genuine environmental issues

Now we've come to the dreaded discussion of the topics about which everyone has an authoritative opinion, but for which no-one has a conclusive answer: global warming, pollution, Armageddon, the Fourth World War (we somehow missed the third one), and other spiky issues.

Before we go on, I will ask you to kindly do me a favour. Let's pretend it's those good old times back in school and we're sitting obediently in a science lesson. There's an exciting experiment I want you to try. Fill a glass with water almost to the top, then gently slide an ice-cube into the glass. Slowly add water to the very rim, using a spoon or a pipette dropper. You can see, the majority of the ice-cube is above the surface. Now, what do you suppose will happen when the ice-cube melts? Will the water overflow onto your table. In fact, although the ice will melt, no water will come over the rim. This is because the density of frozen water is lower than

that of liquid water. Melt the entire Arctic Ocean today, it won't raise the sea level by a millimetre.

Don't get me wrong, we have to do all we can to keep the ice where it is. Still, there are many more environmental issues that also desperately need our attention! (Courtesy Ruud Hein via Creative Commons Licence)

117

This is truly hypothetical and given just by way of an example. I want to keep the Arctic frozen as much as you do. What I really wanted to say was that someone wants to distract you from the real problems by crying about global warming from the top of the bell tower. Global warming is great business. It opens up endless opportunities for greenwashing (a form of unethical business where the marketing effort is based around exploiting peoples' sense of guilt and their soft spot for nature), new taxes and a new level of bureaucracy. A lie can be halfway around the world before the truth gets its boots on. And the truth is that there are far more important problems to tackle than global warming. It's like the recent outcry against butter. If you make people worry about consuming too much of something that has been around for 10,000 years, they may forget about the fact that eating too much junk food and burnt French fries can lead to all sorts of nasty health problems, morbid obesity, and lower life expectancy. But hey, there's some good money to be made in the fast food industry, so why entice the public?

So, what is it that those with vested interests want us to close our eyes to? First and foremost, it's global pollution. There's nothing good in emitting CO_2, but the substance, as you know, is non-toxic. Green plants would die without CO_2. We must cut the CO_2 emissions but we also must tackle other problems. So, plant a tree in your back garden and roll up your sleeves for the following:

Mercury from coal plants

Coal is the most carbon-intensive of the fossil fuels. Almost 1kg of CO_2 is released to generate one kWh of electricity. But CO_2 is not the most dangerous thing that comes out of a coal plant's chimney. 1000kg of coal

A coal plant. Don't be fooled by the white smoke – it contains carbon, mercury, and all sorts of other nasties. (Courtesy Tom Peck from Threaded Thoughts via Creative Commons Licence)

contains on average 0.09 grams of mercury. One gram is enough to pollute a typical 20-acre lake. Of course, not all of the emitted mercury gets into the water system. Some is deposited in the soil, while the remainder is carried through the air for thousands of miles. There is technology to make the coal plants cleaner, but the scientists agree that it won't be used before 2030, when governments will make it obligatory for the coal plants to use emission capture technology.

Paper

Paper is a major reason behind global deforestation. We consume 400 million tons of paper every year, and globally

18 mature trees will be used to make one ton of paper. If only we could be bothered to recycle more. (Courtesy GreenPeace Finland, greenpeace.fi, via Creative Commons Licence)

Where did all the fish go, I'm wondering? (Courtesy Admeiral Crunch via Creative Commons Licence)

only ten per cent of paper is recycled. The fewer trees we have, the harder it will become to fight global warming. The easiest way to stop deforestation is to refuse to buy paper that does not carry an environmental certification. PEFC certification (FSC certificate is also acceptable) is recognized across Europe and means that the paper is sourced from sustainable plantations using environmentally friendly methods. Similar certification applies to other wood-based products; furniture, for instance. An example: two types of printer paper are available from one of the Britain's largest convenience stores. One is of unknown origin, uncertified, and costs £2.08 per 500 sheets. The other one is PEFC certified but costs £2.60. You can afford to spend that extra £0.52 on something that is already super-cheap. It makes a lot of difference!

Untreated sewage and water pollution

Water is a vital part of the planet's environment, and water pollution disrupts the subtle ecosystem and keeps it from restoring itself. Because large amounts of water pollution is generated in agriculture, it might make sense buying organic food. Organic means that no dangerous chemical fertilizers and insecticides are used. Don't expect organic food to have more goodies in it, though.

Battery recycling

Chucking batteries in waste bins is a very shortsighted approach. When the battery casing corrodes away, the

Although the majority of supermarkets are offering a box for battery recycling, too many end up in landfills.
(Courtesy Heather Kennedy via Creative Commons Licence)

chemicals contaminate the soil and ground water. Many shops and stores have introduced battery bins where customers can dispose of their old batteries for free. It is a very convenient way to get rid of unwanted batteries. With the advance of electric cars, global battery production will explode to an unfathomed volume. I am fairly confident that Europe and North America will handle the old batteries properly. Will other countries follow suit?

The icesheet retreat

When it comes to global warming, unfortunately, a significant amount of data supplied to us during the last decade was false. So was the data about pollution. In reality, we've done more damage to the ecosystem than the government wants us to think.

The Earth is constantly undergoing subsequent glaciations and interglaciations – in layman's terms each period of icesheet formation is followed by an icesheet retreat. The latest retreat began when? Did it begin when Henry Ford introduced the conveyor belt, built his model T, and set the precedent of mass CO_2 pollution? No (drum roll) – the latest major retreat began 10,000 years ago, and it will probably go on for another 10,000 years regardless of whether you drive a V8 muscle car or ride a bicycle. We are currently living in a period that is called the Last Ice Age or Quaternary glaciation. According to NASA, a substantial icesheet retreat (although shrinking constantly for the last 10,000 years) began around 1850. Before that there were three hundred years of cold weather (called the Little Ice Age by some scientists). And what happened before that cold spell? You guessed right. From CE 900 to around 1200 there was a period of Medieval Climate Optimum when temperatures were higher. There is a range of methods to reconstruct the climate of the times gone by – geology and archaeology provides enough evidence to back up the theories.

It must be said, though, that this 'global warming' period we live in, shows a steeper temperature increase than the Medieval Climate Optimum. It is more than probable that to a certain extent the temperature increase is due to our activities, but even if we switched off all the powerhouses of the world and went back into caves, we couldn't stop the planet from executing its climate cycle.

While we're on the subject of our activities, methane is even more dangerous greenhouse gas than CO_2, and nobody seems to be fighting the methane emissions. Methane is the ultimate greenhouse gas – 25 times more powerful than CO_2! Much of the methane released into the atmosphere comes from landfills (so let's rethink the way we consume and recycle). According to the Food and Agriculture Organization of the UN, however, more than 30 per cent of the human-caused methane emissions come from farming: manure decomposition and cattle breaking wind! A problem that would be relatively easy to tackle by encouraging farmers to switch to growing vegetables and crops. The rest of it is emitted by various commercial activities and fossil fuel extraction.

Keep in mind that there are enormous amounts of carbon naturally stored in different sources. The ocean, plants and atmosphere contain tens of thousands gigatonnes of carbon. Approximately 300 gigatonnes of CO_2 is released by the ocean each year; plants release 250Gt through respiration, organic rotting generates 200Gt. Human activity contributes only 28Gt. In return, CO_2 is simultaneously absorbed by the green plants and the ocean surface.

The only danger of human-produced CO_2 is that it can upset the subtle gas balance. It's actually much more important to stop polluting the ocean and discourage deforestation, because if the balance between the ocean's natural CO_2 emissions and the atmosphere becomes disrupted, we will be faced with a real CO_2 disaster. The planet has a natural mechanism for restoring itself, and it is capable of doing so on condition that we cut the pollution now!

The length of the periods of substantial glaciations and interglaciations fluctuate between 20,000 and 100,000 years, the most common being 40,000 years. There are so many different factors that can and will affect those fluctuations that it's difficult to even know where to begin: variations in the planet's orbit, type of vegetation, volcanic activity, water exchange between the oceans, configuration of continents, etc. We have to understand the Earth before we jump to conclusions. There are a few possible ways the climate could develop in the future:

• another 300-year long warm period ends around 2150 and global cooling starts
• global warming continues and the Earth becomes ice free, like it was hundreds of millions years ago (we won't live to see it ... it might be tens to hundreds of thousands of years before that happens)
• the current Glacial period continues and deepens making the Earth a snowball like it was some 600 million years ago
• something else happens

So, you see the problem is that the Earth has seen it all before – global warmings and global coolings. We

Switching to energy-saving lightbulbs will shave pounds off your electricity bill, and reduce the environmental impact we're making. (Courtesy Jose Ibarra via Creative Commons Licence)

haven't, and that's why we're panicking. However, if we in our togetherness and wholeness concentrate on the environmental issues that really matter, we stand a chance of creating a good basis of living for generations and generations to come.

The 'green-home-green-car' principle, when a family comes almost entirely off the grid and produces heating and electricity for their home and car is a very big step to take, but I see more and more people considering it a viable option. The greatest task of all is to change the way we consume; step aside from the consumerist attitude we have towards the planet. The change starts with the little things.

Green tips for motorists and fans of Shanks' pony

• Buy and operate only those household appliances that are marked A Class. An A Class washing machine will provide better treatment for your clothes, it will not damage your garments, and you will save energy; lots of energy, in fact. Compare for yourself: an A Class washing machine will use approximately 0.95kW/h in a single washing cycle, while a B Class machine would need 1.15kW/h to do the same job. If you use a C Class washing machine, you burn down 1.3kW/h, or an unbelievable 5.5kW/h if you still operate a G Class or an old unmarked washing machine.

• Use only biodegradable washing powders, and only use those that allow you to wash your laundry at lower temperatures. The modern bio powders provide good results at 30 degrees C. This practice will save you money on electricity, and save money on powder because modern powders are more concentrated and can be used less for the same amount of laundry. You will also reduce global warming and help the planet to recycle the washing powder naturally (as long as it really is biodegradable; check the package before you buy).

• Environmental awareness starts within the family, in your own home. Recycle plastic, glass, and paper whenever possible. It is much cheaper to recycle paper than to produce it from wood pulp. And remember, if you recycle paper, there is a beautiful green tree somewhere that you have saved! You might also wish to review your shopping habits. It is possible that your child doesn't need to upgrade to the latest gadget model twice a year, and maybe you don't need to jump onto a new bit of furniture each time they advertise that huge discount. If you occasionally buy used furniture, not only do you help cut the grey energy, but you also get a chance to find a bit of wooden furniture instead of that chipboard item that will contaminate your home with volatile compounds for the next 20 years.

• When you boil water in your kettle, fill it only with the amount of water necessary; ie, don't boil a full kettle if you're not going to use it. This way you will save energy. It takes only 1kWh of energy to boil two pints of water; to boil three pints you will use almost 1.8kWh.

• Avoid using lifts and elevators. Lifts consume a lot of electricity because they are run by powerful electrical engines. It's not necessary to use an elevator to travel a couple of storeys. Walking up and down the stairs is healthy and helps to train muscles and keeps you fit.

• Consider obtaining a dishwasher. If it's A Class marked, it will use 1kW/h of energy and 25 pints of cold water – a third of the resources that would be spent if washing the same amount of dishes with your hands.

• Don't use a tumble dryer. Ever. Get a clothes line for £0.99 or dry the clothes on radiators.

• We all use chargers. Different types of chargers. We charge our mp3 players, mobile phones, batteries, digital cameras, and other appliances. Some people leave the charger in the socket and it operates around the clock. This is one of the biggest wastes of energy and also accounts for global warming. Touch a charger and you will understand; it's warm, isn't it? When left in a socket it converts energy into heat. An unofficial study in the UK says unattended chargers are wasting around £60,000,000, and more than 100,000 tons of carbon dioxide every year in Britain alone.

• This has been said many times before, but I cannot help reiterating it. Switch off the light when you leave the room. Do not listen to people who say there is a sharp surge of energy consumption when you turn on the light, do not believe those who say that turning on/off frequently damages the light switches and bulbs; none of that is true. Just use the electricity you really need. Don't waste it providing lighting to empty rooms.

• Use energy saving lightbulbs, or even LED light sources instead of the usual incandescent (metal filament) light bulbs. Many countries are planning to ban filament bulbs in the next few years. Energy saving lightbulbs will use only 20 per cent (one fifth) the energy used by a standard lightbulb, and will last ten-15 times longer.

• Choose to support local shops, and never buy food that's travelled from abroad and done high 'food miles.' I bet your country grows tomatoes and produces bread and butter. So why buy these simple everyday things imported from across the ocean? By supporting low 'food miles' produce, you will cut your carbon footprint and boost your local economy.

• Don't leave appliances on standby. According to the Department for Environment Food and Rural Affairs, computers in Britain (both office and home) account for 830GWh of wasted electricity each year, that costs us around £67 million and results in 120,000 tons of unnecessary carbon emissions. These statistics are only for the computers that we use – add the TV sets, DVD players, and extension leads with a signal light and you'll be surprised by the difference.

Index

Save 30%*
on RAC Breakdown Cover.

As a thank you for purchasing your product from RAC, we'd like to offer you 30% off RAC Breakdown Cover.

Here for you 24/7

With RAC you get the peace of mind of knowing we're here to help you 24 hours a day, 365 days a year. We have more patrols per member† than any other breakdown service, so we can find you and fix your problem fast.

If you ever run into trouble on the road, you couldn't be in better hands. And now when you join you'll be better off too, with your 30% discount.

Rest assured with RAC

– Personal based cover – as a driver or passenger in any vehicle**

– Our diagnostic computers start working on your problem from the moment you call

– We aim to reach you within 40 minutes on average and fix 80% of problems on the spot, fast^

– We'll follow you for a while once we've got you going again, just to make sure everything's OK.

To join RAC today for 30% less, call 0800 716 976 and quote DT0440
Calls may be recorded and/or monitored.

or visit rac.co.uk